Praise for the Guide from fashionistas and fashi̇ ▮▮▮▮▮▮▮ professionals

"I know what women wa̧. ⬦ **W9-DJD-234** needs, I feel I am to the needs of women and their jewelry, w... Fashionista's Shopping Guide" is to the needs of women and their shopping".
-Susan Ngo - Jewelry Designer - SparkliesbySusan

"Life's too short to be running around hunting for that perfect pair of shoes to match that dress you will be wearing only once. This book saves me gas and my precious time-which of course is priceless!"
-Rona Casciola - former intimate Apparel Designer, current discount shopping fashionista

"The bible for all price savvy fashionistas. This New York born fashion buyer is keeping this as a permanent fixture in her Louis Vuitton hand bag along with her iPhone and lip gloss. A must to never leave home without it!!!! Amen!"
-Kristen Pizzo - Fashion Buyer

"Sharyne's book is the end all, be all if you have a true "passion for fashion..." So many tips & hints on how to get the best looks for less! A must have for the girl with champagne taste & beer pockets!!!! It's like a little cheat sheet to discount fashion."
-Kim Spatafora - Senior Designer Knits/Sweaters - Perry Ellis

"Every woman should have this shopping guide! Whether you are a local or a tourist this is the only guide you will need. Perfect for the busy gal, you are guaranteed to find yourself some amazing deals."
-Irene Mimnaugh - Fashion Designer - Reunited

"This book is the map that every woman needs to look like a million bucks without spending a million bucks."
- Audra Malone - Technical Designer
Charles Komar and Sons Inc.

THE FASHIONISTA'S SHOPPING GUIDE TO THE GALAXY OF DISCOUNT NEW YORK FASHION

Sharyne Wolfe

The Fashionista's Shopping Guide to the Galaxy of Discount New York Fashion - Copyright 2015 Sharyne Wolfe

ISBN: 145285968X
EAN -13 9781452859682
Cover and interior illustrations: Carmen Gama

ACKNOWLEDGMENTS

I owe special thanks to:
My husband, Mitchel, for his suggestions and his support.

My sister, Bonnie Philo, my partner in shopping "crime" and the "Queen of Canal Street" for her suggestions and tips.

My mother, Joyce B. Schulman, who created two discount shoppingistas.

Karyl Miller for her "fashionista" tips, comments, suggestions and editing advice. I can always count on her sense of humor to enhance any thought.
Karyl Miller and Jack Zabawa, the Photoshop mavins, for formatting the book cover. The book wouldn't have a cover if it wasn't for their efforts.

Kara Brotman, for her legal expertise and editing suggestions.

Carmen Gama who created the cover and interior illustrations for the book. I gave her an overview of what I wanted and her illustrations far exceeded my expectations. And Joseph Pescatore for his tweeking of a mispelling.

My Las Vegas trip cadre: Kara Brotman, Heather Pilibosian and Bonnie Philo for their proofing even after two Margaritas.

Professor Jack Mandel (aka "Dr. JM Love") for his publishing expertise and marketing ideas.

Arlene Mittleman for her proofing expertise.

ABOUT THE AUTHOR

Born and raised in New York City, Sharyne Wolfe is a fashion design graduate of Fashion Institute of Technology. She has a master's degree in Clothing and Textiles from New York University. She has worked in the areas of costume design for Radio City Music Hall, has designed mass market junior sportswear, sold her childrenswear to top Madison Avenue boutiques and designed custom leather clothing for the rock group, Fleetwood Mac. She has also designed shoes and designed handbags that were sold at Bloomingdale's.

Sharyne has been a professor of fashion design for the last twenty-three years and was one of the authors of the design program at Nassau Community College in New York. She has mentored more than one thousand design students who are, or have been, employed in top positions for companies like Tracey Reese, Cynthia Steffe, Cynthia Rowley, Anna Sui, Sears/KMart, Perry Ellis, Victoria's Secret and Derek Lam. One former student had his work featured in a Metropolitan Museum of Art Costume Institute exhibit entitled "Rock Style."

She teaches draping, patternmaking, garment construction, textiles and fashion business practices.

Sharyne's other passion is travel and she has shopped the markets throughout Europe, South America, China, India, South Africa and Southeast Asia. Yet, she still feels that there's no place like home (New York) for shopping deals.

She is a consummate shopper and trolls the stores regularly to unearth the best for less. Her mantra is, "I shop fashion at a discount, therefore I am."

She lives on Long Island with her husband, Mitchel, an architect.

You can contact her at fashionistasshoppingguide@gmail.com

Fashionistas Shopping Guide Website
http://www.fashionistasshoppingguidetodiscountfashion.com

TABLE OF CONTENTS

INTRODUCTION   i

Chapter 1   **DISCOUNT SPECIALTY STORES**   1

Chapter 2   **NOT DISCOUNT BUT...**   17
More bang for your buck

Chapter 3   **DIRECT FROM THE SOURCE**   35
You can get it for
you wholesale

Chapter 4   **SHOES**   39
These boots are made
for walking (or maybe
just for looking fabulous)

Chapter 5   **BLING - NECK, EAR AND WRIST CANDY**   45
Baubles, bangles & beads

FRAGRANCE
Scent of a woman (or man)

MAMA'S GOT A BRAND NEW BAG
(at these prices mama's
got two)

Chapter 6   **HATS - HEAD TRIP**   53
In your Easter bonnet . . .

Chapter 7   **DIAMONDS + GIRLS = BFF**   57
"Square cut or pear shaped,
these rocks don't lose their shape"*

Chapter 8   **HERE COMES THE**   **61**
                        BRIDE

                        A PRINCESS BRIDE
                        Crown her

Chapter 9   **CONSIGNMENT SHOPS**   **67**
                        What goes around
                        comes around

Chapter 10   **VINTAGE**   **79**
                        Everything old is new again

Chapter 11   **THRIFT SHOPS**   **85**
                        The thrill of the hunt

Chapter 12   **CUT FROM THE SAME**   **97**
                        CLOTH
                        Fabric

                        ACCOUTERMENTS
                        Trims, Beads,
                        Feathers, Crystals, etc.

Chapter 13   **ONCE IN A FUCHSIA**   **105**
                        MOON
                        Sometimes sales

Chapter 14   **SAMPLE SALES**   **111**
                        Have I got a deal for you

Chapter 15   **CANAL STREET**   **113**
                        & CHINATOWN
                        Fee-Fi-Faux-Fum,
                        I spy a bag by Louis Vuitton

Chapter 16   **OUTLET STORES**   **119**

Chapter 17   **FASHION JETSETTERS**   **125**
                        Fly me to the stores

Chapter 18 **ESTATE SALES** **127**
They couldn't take it
with them, but you can

**TAG SALES &
GARAGE SALES**
Yours, mine & ours

Chapter 19 **ANYWHERE YOU HANG** **131**
YOUR HAT IS HOME
Hotels in the Big Apple

Chapter 20 **FASHION WEBSITES** **135**
Online shopping
Designer sites
Trend sites

Chapter 21 **FOLLOW THE YELLOW** **142**
BRICK ROAD
Planning your shopping route
Stores and restaurants by area

APPENDIX **CLOTHING SIZE CHART** **160**

INDEX **162**

ORDER FORM **165**

*Diamonds are a Girl's Best Friend" - Gentlemen Prefer Blondes (1953) words by Jule
Styne and music by Leo Robin

"I did not have three thousand pairs of shoes. I had one thousand and sixty."
- Imelda Marcos

INTRODUCTION

Fashion is as old as time itself. In the Garden of Eden, when Eve plucked that fig leaf off of a nearby tree, do you think she debated which leaf was more fashionable or went better with her skin tone? And later, when cave women wrapped themselves in animal skins, do you think there was a social hierarchy based on those who wore squirrel and those who dressed in sable? I do!

Fashion is eternal. Did you know that in the late 1800's in order to achieve the wasp waist that was the fashion of the day, women removed ribs so that they could achieve a 16 inch waist? In the early 1900's, they chained their ankles together to accommodate the narrow circumference at the hem of the hobble skirt.

Women, through time immemorial have strived to be fashionable (well, not all women, but if you're reading this book, I assume you fall into the fashion conscious group).

Fashion is fun and a way to express your personality or mood. You can broadcast whether you're euphoric or down in the dumps by your mode of dress. Or you can counteract your depression and elevate your mood by what you select to wear. Designer Adele Simpson had a fashionable cure for the blues. She suggested, "If you feel blue, wear red!" What sage advice.

Shopping is cheaper than going for analysis (unless of course, you're a shopaholic) and a lot more satisfying. I call it "retail therapy" And at the end of the day you have something to show for it. Who hasn't felt better after finding that perfect pair of Jimmy Choo's (even if they do pinch a bit) or that fabulous sexy dress?

What is your fashion fantasy? Maybe it's wearing the Vivian Westwood wedding gown that Carrie wore in "Sex and the City" or unearthing a Hermes Kelly bag for a $100 or just finding that perfect dress for that special occasion. This book is a guide to winning the fashion lottery

I've compiled this guide for those of you with a passion for fashion, but

i

without the bank account or credit card limit to support it. In the current economic climate where money is tight and job security uncertain, I felt that now more than ever, there was a need for a guide for finding fashion at a discount. Who doesn't want to look like they just walked off the catwalk, but do so at a street smart price? Sure you can shop on the cheap at K-Mart or Kohl's, but for fashion forward women that just doesn't cut it. To paraphrase an old joke:

Question - "What are three words that any fashionable woman will never hear?"

Answer - "Attention K-Mart shoppers."

So voila, I've compiled *"THE FASHIONISTA'S SHOPPING GUIDE TO THE GALAXY OF DISCOUNT NEW YORK FASHION"* for those with Madison Avenue/Couture taste, but without the budget of a trust fund baby.

The Guide was an outgrowth of a accident I had. While at work, I was moving a dress form (the ones you drape patterns on) and the wheels of the form didn't roll, the form stalled and threw me off balance. I fell backwards on my derriere and tried to break my fall with my hand. This turned out to be a bad idea as I broke my right wrist in the process. (Luckily I'm left-handed and this guide was typed with one hand.) I also couldn't drive for eight weeks due to the cast on my arm, since I have a stick shift car. My usual MO is that I would go shopping in my free time. I call it "sport shopping." (Ask around and you'll find that most men don't think it's a viable sport.) So to channel my shopping urge I compiled this guide as a way for me to go virtual shopping until my wrist healed. I hadn't bought anything in five weeks and I was going through withdrawal!

There are other shopping guides to New York City, however, they deal primarily with a store's popularity. I've concentrated on stores that will give you the most bang for your buck. Anyone, (well, almost anyone) can look fabulous shopping at Bergdorf's with an unlimited budget and the help of a personal shopper.

I get more compliments on something that I've bought at a church or estate sale for $2 then I get on an outfit I've splurged on, which led me to compile this guide. Why not share these shopping tips?

The guide is not elitist in its selection of stores. I've included shops that discount $4,000 Chanel jackets and sell them for $750 next to those that sell cute, funky $10 blouses. There are stores listed to fit everyone's budget.

I've also included shops that sell a cross section of styles for different target markets. The stores vary stylewise from the latest cutting edge European imports to the more classic looks of American ready to wear. Whether you're a twenty something trendsetter or a fifty something lover of classic styling, there are alternatives provided.

I've selected both discount and bargain sources in New York City and on Long Island and arranged this shopping guide by category. I've listed mass transit options for each site, if available and suggested using http://www.mapquest.com for driving directions. If you are driving be sure to check the rates at http://www.bestparking.com as they list the lots by area. They give prices for each lot and you can click on many of the lots to get a guaranteed reservation at that rate. Many are a third of the cost of what their regular rate would be. You can also check out http://www.iconparking.com . They have printable coupons for discounted rates for 6/12/24 hours. Parking lots in Manhattan are pricey and wouldn't you rather use that extra cash to buy that cute Miu Miu blouse?

There is a chapter that divides the stores and restaurants by area to make plotting out your day as easy as possible. A little hint about dressing for a day of serious shopping. We all like to look fashionable, however if your shoes pinch, you will not be able to give it your all or be at the top of your game (see it is a sport). When dressing to hit the stores I start with the feet first. Find a comfortable pair of shoes or boots (I do NOT wear sneakers, but that's just me) and coordinate up from there. If all you can think about is, "I can't wait to get these shoes off," you will not be at your shopping best.

Fashion is food for the soul, but we still need food for the body. So, to nourish your body and kick start your energy level, I've noted restaurants in a number of the listings. Any restaurant I've listed, I've eaten in. In 2010, the New York City Health Department instituted a grading system for restaurants. These letter grades ranging from A through C must be posted in restaurant's window and are based on cleanliness.

If I don't list an eatery, you're on your own. In a pinch, you usually can't go wrong with pizza. After all, it has three or four of the six food groups - grains, vegetables and milk. Add pepperoni and you include the meat group. I also pack a power bar or almonds in my bag, if I should feel peckish. Both are good energy boosters.

And when you've got to go, you've got to go. I've listed sources for a bathroom break in a number of areas.

As shopping is a large part of a trip to New York, I've geared this guide to both native New Yorkers and visitors to the Big Apple. While some of the information may seem obvious to a denizen of Murray Hill, those visiting from London or Tokyo will find it helpful. I've included a chapter to guide those visitors to finding the best hotel at a reasonable price.

And finally, this guide was compiled in much the manner as "Consumer Reports". No entry in the guide has paid to be included. These are all my own picks.

I've always said that you can find anything in New York and usually at a better price than anywhere else in the world, **IF** you know where to shop. For those of you who have more panache than cash this guide is for you.

I'd like to bid a fond farewell to Filene's Basement that closed its doors in December 2011 after 102 years. The Filene's "Running of the Brides" is no longer. Sym's another off price retailer also shut its business after 50 years. And Daffy's bit the dust after 25 years on the fashion scene. Finally a fond adieu to the grandmommy of discounters, Loehmann's. After 93 years, they are no longer.

I would love both feedback to the entries and suggestions for future inclusions. fashionistasshoppingguide@gmail.com
For updates on the latest sales, deals, events and fashion news, check out my website at
http://www.fashionistasshoppingguidetodiscountfashion.com
Happy shopping and may all of your fashion cravings be fulfilled.

"A dress makes no sense unless it inspires men to take it off you."
- Francoise Sagen - French writer

YOU ARE A FASHIONISTA:

1.   if you immediately wonder "what will I wear?" no matter what the occasion.

2.   if people constantly ask you, "where did you get that great... ?"

3.   if your motto is, "A day without shopping is like a day without sunshine."

4.   if your closet is filled to bursting and to make more room you bought those skinny hangers.

5.   if instead of counting sheep to fall asleep, you coordinate outfits.

6.   if you wear the perfect outfit to shop for the perfect outfit.

7.   if you have three-year-old sweaters in your dresser with the tags still on them.

8.   if you have an orgasm when you hear the words "walk-in closet."

9.   if your husband's only closet is in the basement.

10.   if when you go on a trip, you have three pieces of luggage to his one.

11.   if you shop till you drop.

12.   if you don't know how many pairs of shoes you have.

YOU ARE A DISCOUNT SHOPPINGISTA:

1.   if you almost never pay full price.

2.   if your heart races at the mention of a 50% off sale.

3.   if when entering a store you go straight for the discount racks.

4.   if you're wearing an outfit comprising a Marc Jacobs' dress and shoes from Prada and it cost less than $100 ($50 is even better).

5.   if you have twelve pairs of black shoes, because they were all such a deal.

6.   if you buy one to get one free, but you really don't want the free one.

7.   if you give up lunch with the girls, their treat, for a 60% off sale and for a 75% off midnight madness sale . . . , well, let's just say your date will wait.

8.   if you're suffering from the flu but your favorite store is having its annual 75% off sale, and you drag your sick body out of bed, put on some makeup (you look terrible) and hustle over.

9.   if you buy holiday and birthday gifts for friends and family when you see them at a great price in February, put them away and then can't find them.

10.   if you've lost track of how many black blazers you have and you continue to buy them because they were such a bargain.

11.   if, for family and close friends, you leave the tag with the discounted price on their gift because they will appreciate the deal you got.

12.   if playing the "you'll never guess what it cost me game" is more satisfying that the actual purchase.

FASHION TIPS 101

1.   BUT IT WAS SUCH A GREAT DEAL . . .

Remember it's not a bargain unless you wear it. Sure that $1500 Moschino dress marked down to $20 is a steal, but if you're not the 1% of the population that looks good in chartreuse it's not a smart buy. Don't buy it just because it's on sale.

2.   BUT, IT WILL FIT IF . . .

Work with the attributes that you have.
Don't buy something that will fit you when:

> you lose five pounds.
> you gain five pounds.
> you grow three inches.
> you get lipo.
> you get a boob job.
> you get a breast reduction.

It doesn't work.

3.   IF THE DRESS FITS

Buy what fits! If it needs minor alterations like a hem, it's not a problem. But if it requires a pinch here and a tuck there, your discount price suddenly evaporates, unless you can do the alterations yourself.

4.   CLOSET CANDY

We've all done this. You love that dress; it's to die for and the price is unbelievable. You buy it and it sits in your closet taking up room, which most of us don't have to spare. There was something about it that just didn't work, maybe you had nowhere you could wear it, or you couldn't get the look together but this garment turned into closet candy (eye candy for your closet). You may as well frame it and hang it on your wall.

5.   BUT IT FIT IN THE STORE

You find these amazing shoes at an unbelievable price. You try them on and they fit like a glove. But the first time you actually wear them they rub, pinch or chaff. What happened?

Maybe you tried them on after a hard day of shopping and your feet had swelled. Or you gave the shoes the benefit of the doubt, because you adored them. I bought a pair of gold ankle strap Manolo's with three inch heels at a garage sale for $25. They were perfect for a dress I was going to wear New Year's eve. When I tried them on, they fit and they were such a deal. But, by the time the clock struck midnight, I could barely walk and I was the only one who really knew they were Manolo's. I put them on Ebay rather than hobble around and I hope the woman in Hawaii had better luck with them than I did. Hint: Make sure you take those swollen tootsies into account when trying on shoes.

6. IF YOU HAVEN'T WORN IT IN A YEAR, GET RID OF IT . . . NOT

Personally, I don't subscribe to this axiom. I have great pieces that I haven't worn in five years, resurrect them from the bowels of my closet and a star is born. I have a white eyelet flared and gathered skirt that I bought over a decade ago. It's a basic skirt, so it doesn't scream 1998. I've done a pick up on the side with a silk flower pin and it feels new. In fact, a saleslady in one of the Upper East side consignment shops wanted to know who the designer was.

7. SHOPPING WITH A FRIEND IS A DOUBLE EDGE SWORD

Sure it's fun to shop in packs, but opinions can be invaluable or worthless. Know your shopping buddy. Is her (or his) taste in line with yours? A good friend who tells you that those pants accentuate your muffin top is a valuable asset. But one that encourages you to buy that slinky knit dress that is her taste, not yours, is not. Be forewarned if you shop with a friend whose size and style match yours you may end up fighting her for the last pair of marked down Jimmy Choo's. Lesser situations have torn friendships asunder.

8. NEVER GO SHOPPING WITH YOUR SIGNIFICANT OTHER OR SPOUSE

In my experience, and that of most of the women I know, shopping with a spouse or significant other usually spells trouble. Do they really have the patience to wade through racks of merchandise, sit without complaining while you try on a dozen pairs of shoes and when you ask their opinion, not say "That looks great" to the first item you try on, just to get out of the store? Some men are great at shopping, but they are few and far between.

9.   DRESS YOUR AGE?

I don't fully agree with this premise. Sure if you're 70, you shouldn't dress like a 15 year old and wear midriff baring tops and low-cut jeans. (I actually have seen 15 year olds that shouldn't be decked out in that outfit.) I worked with a woman who at 75 had fabulous legs. She wore short skirts to show them off, not skirts that "let it all hang out " and gave you a glimpse of what she had for breakfast, but they were short and she looked great. Look at Tina Turner. Why should age dictate your clothing style? Select your wardrobe with common sense.

10.   KNOW THYSELF, BUT . . .

To thine own self be true, but . . .   Just because it's in fashion, it doesn't mean you should be in it. We all have our personal style. We tend to gravitate toward a certain look. Whether you are Connie conservative, Susan sexy or Tricia trendy, you know where your fashion strength lies. But, what if Connie conservative wants to be Susan sexy when she goes out clubbing. Surprise people. Fashion should be fun; by dressing in a certain manner, you can play a part. Who wants to be the same, same day after day? Mix it up a bit.

11.   TRY IT ON, YOU NEVER KNOW

Not every size eight fits the same.   Each designer sizes their collections for their target market. A Donna Karan size eight is more of a size six and a Jones NY size eight is cut like a size 10. I've worn everything from a zero to a size 10 (not because of weight fluctuations) depending on the company. Don't necessarily go by the size, try it on. Interestingly enough, I've found this recently with shoes. I found a fabulous size 6-1/2 pair of black heels with toe cleavage that laced around the ankle. I'm a 7-1/2 or eight, but this 6-1/2 fit.

So give it a shot, you never know. And, if the shoe fits, buy it!

A DISCOUNT SHOPPER IS BORN

Once upon a time there was a little girl from Brooklyn who had champagne taste and a beer budget, or, putting it more in the universe of a 7-year-old, a triple scoop hot fudge sundae with lots of whipped cream taste (yum) and a popsicle budget.

Growing up in Brooklyn in a middle class household, my mother always looked to save when buying clothing for me and my sister. She was a woman with a mission. She wanted us to look nice, but couldn't afford to outfit us at Saks or Bergdorf's. To get the best for the least, my mother used to shop the sales. J.W. May's Department store on Fulton Street in Brooklyn, held a twice yearly children's sample coat sale, in February for Spring and in August for Fall. They used to sell sample coats from all the best childrenswear houses for $12. These coats would normally sell for $50 at the shops on Fifth Avenue. We'd take the subway to downtown Brooklyn; the goal was to get a Rothschild coat (THE coat to have) for a fraction of its initial price. This early experience got me hooked on getting great clothes at a discount price. My mother wanted her daughters to look like a million dollars (or if adjusted for today's inflation, five hundred million dollars) but at the right price.

To make the clothing budget stretch further, my mother sewed some of our outfits, including big sister/little sister looks. She also sewed outfits for some of the girls in the neighborhood, using the same fabric so that often we looked like we were wearing garments bought at a fire sale. When I was seven, I thought this was neat, but by 11, the novelty had worn off.

As I grew into a preteen and discovered big girl clothes, my mother got a little more creative. The scenario went like this. I would go into the top stores and pick out my school wardrobe and then my mother would try to get it wholesale. This would involve a number of clever ruses. If the company was listed on the stock exchange, she would call them and say that at the last stockholder's meeting she attended, (which she didn't), Mr. So and So said that as a stockholder, (which she wasn't), she should just call the company and they would accommodate her. She related this story to one company whose response was, "You were at the stockholder's meeting in Bermuda?" It was obvious that a little more research had to be done when using this ploy.

Another tactical maneuver involved calling the selected company and telling them that when she recently spoke with Mr. Goldberg (a name she pulled out of thin air), he said it would be fine for her to come up and buy wholesale. The response by one company was, "Mr. Goldberg died." Whoops! Time to check the obits.

But most times, we'd be able to go up to the company in Manhattan, give them the style numbers and pick up what we ordered from their shipping department. At that time, most of the shipping was done from Seventh Avenue, so I was always in fashion.

As discounters came on the shopping scene, and I started shopping on my own, I discovered a whole world of options for getting the most for the least.

And in the end, the little girl with champagne taste and a beer budget found her niche as a fashion discount shopper and she lived happily ever after . . . in Chanel (bought at a consignment shop), Manolo's (bought at a garage sale) and Moschino (bought at Century 21).

CHAPTER 1

DISCOUNT SPECIALTY STORES

"Clothes make the man. Naked people have little or no influence on society."
Mark Twain

DISCOUNT SPECIALTY STORES

CENTURY 21 DEPARTMENT STORES
The Holy Grail of Discount Shopping
http://www.c21stores.com
Sign up at their website for the occasional percentage off coupon.

The Holy Grail of discount shopping!!!!!!!!! Their original NYC store was destroyed on 9/11 along with the World Trade Center, but they rebuilt at Cortlandt Street. Though it sounds like a real estate firm, they carry everything from designer men's, women's and children's clothing, accessories, linens, luggage and lingerie. Shoes that will make your feet dance. Their motto is "fashion worth fighting for." (And, on occasion, fights have broken out). I've gotten everything from Chanel scarves (for $80) though that's rare, to La Perla bras and Dolce & Gabanna. Typically they carry Pucci, Juicy, Marc Jacobs, Paul Smith, Vivienne Westwood, Lanvin, Save the Queen, ABS, Sue Wong, Moschino, Prada, Miu, Miu, Gaultier, to name just a sampling. They have a fashion forward mix, catwalk chic fashion and a fabulous European designer department. They do also carry top American designers, Calvin, Ralph, Michael, and Donna. Their everyday prices are 50%-75% off retail.

They also carry housewares, decorative home accessories, luggage, and cosmetics.

The best time to shop there is after Christmas or at the end of a season, as they drop their already discounted prices another 65% to 80%.
Return policy - 30 days with tags attached and receipt - they are quite strict about this.

NOTE - They're closed on Rosh Hashana and Yom Kipper. Check your calendar as the dates vary from year to year, but are usually in September or October.

LOCATIONS
For driving directions check http://www.mapquest.com

For discount parking check out http://www.bestparking.com and http://www.iconparking.com

<u>Manhattan</u>
22 Cortlandt Street between Broadway & Church Streets
212-227-9092.
> <u>Mass transit</u>
> R, W - Cortlandt Street

Lincoln Square
1972 Broadway between 66th and 67th Streets
212-518-2121
> <u>Mass transit</u>
> #1 - West 66th Street - Lincoln Center

<u>Brooklyn</u>
472 86th Street between 4th & 5th Avenues
718-748-3266
> <u>Mass transit</u>
> R - 86th Street

<u>Queens</u>
61-01 Junction Boulevard
718-699-2121
> <u>Mass transit</u>
> R, V, G - 63rd Drive

<u>Westbury, Long Island</u>
1085 Old Country Road
516-333-5200

> <u>Restaurants</u>
> Westbury
> Café Baci
> http://www.cafebaci.com
> 1636 Old Country Road
> 516-832-8888
> Baci is a few minutes west of Century 21. It's impossible to get a table on a weekend evening without waiting for 1-1/2 hours. Lunch is better though. Absolutely HUGE portions of

delicious pasta. Share!

For a faster meal in the same strip mall as Century, try Mama Teresa's. You can grab a slice or have a full meal.

FOX'S
http://www.foxs.com/index.htm

Fox's has been around for over 20 years. Their motto is, "The thrill of a great buy." They sell brand name apparel from top designers at off-prices. Some locations also sell shoes. I don't shop there often, but have found that they have an interesting merchandise mix. I have discovered some diamonds in the rough. Their location in Huntington is well laid out and easy to shop.
Return policy
3 days with tags attached and receipt - full refund.

LOCATIONS
For driving directions check http://www.mapquest.com

Manhattan
2234 Broadway at 80th Street
212-362-8409
> Mass transit
> #1 - 79th Street

Brooklyn
911-927 Kings Highway
718-645-3620
> Mass transit
> F - Avenue P

Forest Hills, Queens
70-39 Austin Street
718-261-4100
> Mass transit
> E, F - Forest Hills - this is not very close though.

Mineola, Long Island
80 Main Street
(Shoes/Accessories)
79 Main Street
516-294-8321
> Mass transit
> LIRR - Mineola
>
> Restaurant
> Grimaldi's Pizza
> http://www.grimaldisrestaurant.com
> 980 Franklin Avenue
> Garden City
> 516-294-6565
> Down the road a piece, (just a mile), Grimaldi's is the Garden City branch of the famed Brooklyn eatery. Crispy brick oven pizza and pastas served with your selection of toppings. It gets very crowded and the wait for a table in the evening can exceed an hour. So go at off times or early to avoid the crush.

Huntington, Long Island
379 New York Avenue
631-424-5221

> Restaurant
> Black & Blue Seafood Chophouse
> http://www.blackandbluehuntington.com/
> 65 Wall Street
> Huntington
> 631-385-9255
> Terrific lunches and dinner, both fish and meat selections.. They have a $28.95 three course prix fixe menu at dinner and sandwiches and wraps at lunch. They also have a gluten free menu.

T.J. MAXX
http://www.tjmaxx.com

Their website states, "Where fashionistas become Maxxinistas."

T.J. Maxx carries a diverse range of men's, women's and children's clothing, shoes and accessories in addition to decorative home accessories and housewares.

I've picked up great designer swimsuits here at a decidedly non-designer price.

Some stores have a section called "Runway" and have upscale designers such as, Roberto Cavalli, Stella McCartney and Tory Burch.

You can also find some very reasonable baubles, bangles and beads in their jewelry department.

Return policy
30 days with receipt - full refund.
Over 30 days or no receipt - store credit.

LOCATIONS
For driving directions check http://www.mapquest.com
For discount parking check out http://www.bestparking.com and http://www.iconparking.com

Check their website for additional locations.

Manhattan
620 Avenue of The Americas at 18th Street
212-229-0875

> Mass transit
> #1 -18th Street
> F, V - 14th Street
>
> Restaurant
> Le Pain Quotidien
> 38 East 19th Street between Broadway & Park Avenues
> 212-673-7900
> Healthy fare served. Interesting tartines, soups, salads.

Columbus Village
808 Columbus Ave near 100th Street
212-222-0543
> Mass transit
> #1, 2, 3, B, C - 96th Street

14 Wall Street
212-587-8459
> Mass Transit
> #2, 3, 4, 5 - Wall Street
> J, Z - Broad Street

250 West 57th Street
212-245-6201
> Mass Transit
> #1, 2, A, B, C, D - 59th Street - Columbus Circle
> N, Q, R - 57th Street - 7th Avenue
> B, D, E - 7th Avenue

Bridgemarket
407 East 59th Street
212-486-2142
> Mass Transit
> N, Q, R - Lexington Avenue - 59th Street
> #4, 5, 6, 7, 7X - 59th Street

Brooklyn
502 86th St between 5th Avenue & Gelston Avenue
718-759-9830
> Mass Transit
> R - 86th Street
> R - Bay Ridge - 95th Street

Kingswood Center
1630 East 15th Street
718-336-1194
> Mass transit
> B, Q - Kings Highway

Bronx
New Horizons Shopping Center
174th Street & Vyse Avenue
718-378-5780

1 Fordham Plaza
718-933-8790
>Mass transit
>Metro North - Fordham

Rego Park, Queens
Rego Park Center
6101 Junction Boulevard
718-271-8457
>Mass transit
>G, R, - 63rd Road

College Point, Queens
136-03 20th Avenue
718-353-2727

Staten Island
1509 Forest Avenue
718-876-1995

New Hyde Park, Long Island
2315 New Hyde Park Road
516-327-5967

Carle Place, Long Island
Parkway Plaza
217 Glen Cove Road
516-873-2522

Greenvale, Long Island
90 Northern Boulevard
516-625-2530

>Restaurants
>Cucina Centro

43 Glen Cove Road - Greenvale
516-484-3880
Less than five minutes away. Try their thin crust pizza or pear salad. Share a portion of pasta.

Sarin Thai
http://www.sarinthaicusine.com
43 Glen Cove Road
Greenvale
516-484-5873
In the same strip mall as Centro, Sarin offers an inexpensive lunch menu of fresh Thai specialties.

Red Mango - closed
http://www.redmangousa.com
Wheatley Plaza - Greenvale
350 Wheatley Plaza
516-801-0510
Located in the strip mall one block east. For a quick pick-me-up, try Red Mango's frozen yoghurt with a choice of toppings.

Hicksville, Long Island
The Woodbury Shopping Center
410 South Oyster Bay Road
516-433-4880

Restaurant
Pasta-eria
440 South Oyster Bay Road
Hicksville
516-938-1555
In the same shopping center as T.J. Maxx. Pasta and pizza. Share. The portions are large.

Commack, Long Island
5020 Jericho Turnpike
631-462-2610

MARSHALLS
http://www.marshallsonline.com/

Shoportunities abound (as they spout in their print and media ads). A seller of discount fashion, Marshalls carries men's, women's and children's clothing, shoes and accessories, in addition to home fashions and gourmet food.

When Marshalls came on the scene, years ago, it was my favorite place to buy underwear.

It's a hit or miss proposition and you're just as likely to hit a home run (okay, maybe a double) as to strike out. Shopping here requires persistence. But, if you need cute underwear . . .

Return policy
30 days with receipt - full refund.
No receipt - the lowest selling price in a gift card.

LOCATIONS
For driving directions check http://www.mapquest.com
For discount parking check out http://www.bestparking.com and http://www.iconparking.com

Check their website for additional locations..

Manhattan
Harlem Center
125 West 125th Street between Seventh & Lenox Avenues
212-866-3963
> Mass transit
> #2, 3 - 125th Street

East River Plaza
517 East 117th Street, Ste 401
917-492-2892

620 Avenue of Americas between 18th and 19th Streets
212-741-0621
> Mass Transit
> F, M - 14th Street
> #1, 2 - 18th Street
> L - 6th Avenue

Brooklyn
Atlantic Center
625 Atlantic Avenue
718-398-5254
> Mass transit
> #2, 3, 4, 5, M, N, Q, W, R, B, D - Atlantic Avenue - Pacific St.
> C - Lafayette Avenue
> G - Fulton Street

1832 86th Street
718-621-3434
> Mass transit
> B, M - 18th Street

Brooklyn Gateway Center
351 Gateway Drive
718-235-8142

1623 Avenue Y
718-934-4570

Rego Park, Queens
96-05 Queens Boulevard
718-275-7797
> Mass transit
> G, R - 63rd Street - Rego Park

Ozone Park, Queens
9210 Rockaway Boulevard
718-845-6870
> Mass transit
> A - 88th Street - Boyd Avenue

Jamaica, Queens
168-23 Jamaica Avenue
718-725-0409
>Mass transit
>E, J, Z - Jamaica Center

Flushing, Queens
Sky View Center
40-24 College Point Boulevard
718-463-2537
>Mass transit
>#7 - Flushing

Long Island City, Queens
4818 Northern Boulevard
718-626-4700
>Mass transit
>G, R, V - 46th Street

Bronx
Bay Plaza Shopping Center
2100 Bartow Avenue
718-320-7211

River Plaza
50 West 225th Street
718-933-9062
>Mass transit
>Metro North - Marble Hill
>#1, 9 - 231st Street

The Shops at Bruckner Boulevard
845 White Plains Road
718-597-3071

Gateway Center - 610 Exterior Street
718-292-6319
>Mass transit
>#3 - 145th Street (you have to cross the 145th Street bridge)

Elmont, Long Island
Elmont Shopping Center
600 Hempstead Turnpike
516-354-4475

Westbury/Carle Place, Long Island
1240 Old Country Road
516-683-1078

> Restaurant
> Café Baci
> 1636 Old Country Road
> Westbury
> See description on page 3.

Lawrence, Long Island
Bay Harbour Mall
Rockaway Turnpike
516-239-5100

Massepequa, Long Island
5500 Sunrise Highway
516-799-5201

Manhasset, Long Island
1380 Northern Boulevard
516-627-5492

> Restaurants
> Cipollini
> http://www.cipolinnirestaurant.com
> The Americana Manhasset
> 2110C Northern Boulevard off Searingtown Road
> 516-627-7172
> For lunch try their thin crust pizza or a salad. A bit pricey
> though.
>
> Joanne's Gourmet Pizza
> http://www.kpsearch.com/DF/Joannes/all.asp
> 1067 Northern Boulevard, Roslyn

Joanne's is about five minutes east of Marshalls. A large selection of great pizza for a quick pick me up prior to hitting the stores again.

Jericho, Long Island
499 Broadway
516-433-8553

Restaurant
Sawa Sushi
http://www.sawacuisine.com
260 Jericho Turnpike
Syosset
516-496-8886
Sawa is a favorite of mine. Great bento boxes, imaginative rolls and melt in your mouth sashimi. It's about a five minute drive from Marshalls.

Huntington, Long Island
Big H Shopping Center
839 New York Avenue
631-271-7339

New Hyde Park, Long Island
1484 Union Turnpike
516-328-0132

ANNIE SEZ
http://www.anniesez.com/

Their tag line is, "It's not just a store, it's an obsession." Bridge line sportswear and some designer names at 20% to 60% off department store prices.

Go to their website for percent off coupons. Their merchandise is a mix of basics, with some trendy items thrown in. Check out their 50% and 70% off racks for a real deal. They carry shoes and accessories too.

Return policy

30 days with receipt on regular price merchandise - full refund.
14 days with receipt on 25% or 50% off merchandise - full refund.
70% off - final sale.
No receipt - merchandise credit at lowest selling price.

LOCATIONS

For driving directions check http://www.mapquest.com

Brooklyn
6401 18th Avenue
718-234-8057
Mass transit
N - 18th Avenue

2067 Coney Island Avenue
718-376-2609
Mass transit
F - Kings Highway

Queens
9210 Rockaway Boulevard
718-845-0679

Staten Island
2530 Hylan Boulevard & 430 New Dorp Lane
718-351-7675

Glen Cove, Long Island
121 School Street Space 75
516- 609-2607

Merrick, Long Island
1630-34 Merrick Road & Chernucha Avenue
516-377-4512

Plainview, Long Island
377 South Oyster Bay Road
516- 822-4646

<u>Restaurant</u>
Pasta-eria
440 South Oyster Bay Road
Hicksville
See description on page 9.

CHAPTER 2

NOT DISCOUNT BUT . . .
More bang for your buck

"Be sure what you want and be sure about yourself. Fashion is not just beauty, it's about good attitude. You have to believe in yourself and be strong."
-Adriana Lima

NOT DISCOUNT BUT . . .
More bang for your buck

These stores are not discounters, but they do offer fashion, albeit, sometimes disposable, at throwaway prices. I've uncovered some real treasures and if I only wear them for one season, at these prices, c'est la vie.

H&M
http://www.hm.com

H&M (Hennes & Mauritz), a Swedish company, operates in 37 countries and has more than 74,000 employees.

For the last few years, they've enlisted top designers to create limited collections for the store. Among them Jimmy Choo, Karl Lagerfeld, Viktor & Rolf, Stella McCartney, and Comme des Garcons These are carried in select stores and usually sell out in a New York minute. Often the fashion savvy line up the night before the launch date to snag a designer item at a decidedly non-designer price.

A discriminating shopper can separate the wheat from the chaff and uncover a treasure.

I purchased a long black "down" coat at H&M a few years ago that I just love. I was in Chanel (just looking) and the salesman wanted to know who the designer was.

Their "The Garden Collection" is made with environmentally adapted materials like recycled polyester, organic cotton and organic linen.
Return policy
30 days with receipt - full refund.
Over 30 days or no receipt - store credit at current selling price.

LOCATIONS
For driving directions check http://www.mapquest.com
For discount parking check out http://www.bestparking.com and http://www.iconparking.com

They have 20 locations in New York City and on Long Island. I've listed a representation. Check their website for additional stores.

<u>Manhattan</u>
111 Fifth Avenue at 18th Street
212- 539-1741

<u>Mass transit</u>
F - 14th Street

<u>Restaurant</u>
Le Pain Quotidien
38 East 19th Street between Broadway & Park Avenue
212-673-7900
See description on page 6.

1328 Broadway at 34th Street
646-473-1165

<u>Mass transit</u>
B, D, F, N, Q, R, V, W - 34th Street

<u>Restaurant</u>
Pret a Manger
1020 Avenue of the Americas at 38th Street
646-688-1061
I love this place for a quick sandwich or salad. They do interesting combos and you can buy half a sandwich, if you're watching your girlish figure.

150 East 86th Street & Lexington Avenue
212-289-1724

<u>Mass transit</u>
#4, 5, 6 - East 86th Street

<u>Restaurant</u>
Le Pain Quotidien
1131 Madison Avenue between 84th & 85th Streets
212-327-4900
See description on page 6.

435 Seventh Avenue at 34th Street

212- 643-6955

Mass transit
#1 - 34th Street

Restaurants
Pret a Manger
485 Seventh Avenue
646-360-1625
Closed Saturday & Sunday
See description on page 19.

Café Metro
530 Seventh Avenue at 38th Street
212-398-8788
Cafeteria style restaurant serving soups, salads, sandwiches, wraps, pizza.

505 Fifth Avenue at 42nd Street

212- 661-7012

Mass transit
#7 - 5th Avenue

Restaurant
Bryant Park Grill
http://www.arkrestaurants.com
25 West 40th Street
212-840-6500
A lovely setting, but a bit pricey. Great salads.

640 Fifth Avenue & 51st Street

212 489-0390

Mass transit
#4 , 6, V - Lexington Avenue - 53rd Street
V - 5th Avenue - 53rd Street

731 Lexington Avenue and 59th Street

212-935-6781

Mass transit
#4, 5, 6 - 59th Street

N, R - Lexington Avenue

<u>Restaurant</u>
40 Carrots @ Bloomingdale's
Lexington & 59th Street
Great for a salad or sandwich. Try their frozen yoghurt

4 Times Square - 1472 Broadway
855-466-7467
<u>Mass transit</u>
#7 - Times Square

<u>Soho</u>
558 Broadway
212-343-2722
515 Broadway between Spring and Broome Streets
212-965-8975
<u>Mass transit</u>
#6 - Bleeker Street

<u>Restaurant</u>
Lure
http://www.lurefishbar.com
142 Mercer Street off Prince Street
212-431-7676
Down a flight of steps this fish bar has a great brunch menu.
Order their sushi or a salad at lunch.

<u>Brooklyn</u>
Kings Plaza Mall
5100 Kings Plaza
718-252-5444
<u>Mass transit</u>
B, Q - Newkirk Avenue

<u>Elmhurst, Queens</u>
Queens Center Mall
90-15 Queens Boulevard
718-592-4200

Mass transit
G, R, V - Woodhaven Boulevard

Garden City, Long Island
Roosevelt Field Mall
Old Country Road
516-294-0535

Hicksville, Long Island
Broadway Mall
906 Broadway
855-466-7467

Westbury
Mall at the Source - 1504 Old Country Road
855-466-7467

Restaurant
Café Baci
http://www.cafebaci.com
1636 Old Country Road
516-832-8888
See description on page 3.

FOREVER 21
http://www.forever21.com

I've dubbed Forever 21 (XXI Forever), the kingdom of knock-offs. Though not known for it's impeccably made designer clothing, Forever 21 has a knack for turning out a dead on copy of top designer fashion. The fashion industry routinely offers inexpensive versions of current designer fashions, but Forever 21 seems to be almost picture perfect with their copies. So much so that they've been sued by Diane Von Furstenberg, Anthropologie, and Anna Sui. A few years ago, DVF's $325 "Cerisier" smock, was renamed "Sabrina" and sold by Forever 21 for $32. The dresses were identical, down to not only the pattern, color and measurements, but both were made of 100 percent silk. Looking at the two side by side, I'd be hard pressed to distinguish which was which.

They have recently upgraded their collections, adding additional labels like Heritage 1981, B19, Twelve by Twelve. They have even added a line called Faith 21 (extended sizes) for those who do not wear a size XS. Their styling is fun and flirty and their prices are bargain-basement.

And now fashionable men need not feel deprived as there is a men's department featuring the latest fashions.

You don't have to be 21 to wear their clothing. So, whether you're young or young at heart, if you crave that very trendy item whose shelf life date is set to expire by Tuesday, Forever 21 is a good place to shop. Sure, they're not made to last, but at these prices, who cares? Fashion is fleeting, right?

Check website for additional locations.

Return policy

21 days with tags and receipt - store credit.

Sale items - final sale.

LOCATIONS

For driving directions check http://www.mapquest.com

For discount parking check out http://www.bestparking.com and http://www.iconparking.com

Manhattan

50 West 34th Street & Broadway

212-564-2346

Mass transit

B, D, F, N, Q, R, V, W - 34th Street

40 East 14th Street - Broadway & University Place

212-228-0598

Mass transit

#4, 5, 6, L, N, Q, R, W - 14th Street - Union Square

Restaurant

Tocqueville.

1 East 15th Street

212- 647-1515

An elegant restaurant that offers a prix fixe three course lunch for $29.00.

Times Square - 1540 Broadway at 45th Street
212-302-0594

Mass Transit
S - Times Sq - 42nd Street
N, R, Q - 49th Street
B, D, F, M - 47th - 50th Streets - Rockefeller Center

Soho
568 Broadway between Houston & Prince Streets
212-941-5949

Mass transit
R - Prince Street

Restaurant
Lure
142 Mercer Street off Prince Street
212-431-7676
See description on page 21.

Brooklyn
Kings Plaza Shopping Center
5301 Kings Plaza between Flatbush Avenue & Avenue Q
718-434-0781

Mass transit
B, Q - Newkirk Avenue

Queens Center - Elmhurst
90-15 Queens Boulevard between 57th & 59th Avenues
718-699-5630

Mass transit
G, R, V - Woodhaven Boulevard

Staten Island
Staten Island Mall
2655 Richmond Ave between Platinum Avenue & Richmond Hill Road
718-477-2121

Garden City, Long Island
Roosevelt Field Mall
630 Old Country Road #1124A
516-873-9379

Hicksville, Long Island
Broadway Mall
603A Broadway Mall
516-681-1460

> Restaurant
> Chipotle
> 215 N Broadway - Hicksville
> 516-822-4074
> Directly across from the Broadway Mall Chipotle serves fresh "choose your own ingredients" foil wrapped, handcrafted, local farm supporting burritos and other Mexican favorites. Yummy guacamole.

Valley Stream, Long Island
Green Acres Mall
2034 Green Acres Mall, Space #108
516-256-0700

STRAWBERRY
http://www.aestores.com/home.asp?p=stores

The first Strawberry stores have been around since the era of YSL's peasant collection. They carry inexpensive trendy items. Don't expect any service, but for a cheap trend fix, it's a good place to go.
Return policy
10 days with tags attached and receipt - full refund.
Over 10 days with tags attached and receipt - store credit.
Sale items - final sale.

LOCATIONS
For driving directions check http://www.mapquest.com
For discount parking check out http://www.bestparking.com and http://www.iconparking.com

Check website for additional locations

<u>Manhattan</u>
129 East 42nd Street at Lexington Avenue
212-986-7030
> <u>Mass transit</u>
> #4, 5, 6, 7 - 42nd Street - Grand Central
>
> <u>Restaurant</u>
> Sbarro
> http://www.sbarro.com/
> 451 Lexington Avenue between 44th & 45th Streets
> Pizza, pasta, salads. Great for a fast refuel.

286 First Avenue at 17th Street
212-.677-4986
> <u>Mass transit</u>
> #4, L, R, N, Q, S - 14th Street

14 West 34th Street off Fifth Avenue
212-279-8696
> <u>Mass transit</u>
> B, D, F, N, Q, R - 34th Street
>
> <u>Restaurant</u>
> Sbarro
> 159 West 33rd Street at Seventh Avenue
> See description on page 26.

38 East 14th Street at Broadway
212-353-2700
> <u>Mass transit</u>
> #4, 5, 6, L, N, R -14th Street - Union Square
>
> <u>Restaurant</u>
> Tocqueville.
> 1 East 15th Street
> 212- 647-1515
> See description on page 23.

49 West 57th Street bet. Fifth Avenue & Avenue of the Americas
212-688-0348
> Mass transit
> B, Q, N, R - 57th Street
>
> Restaurant
> Red Eye Grill
> http://www.redeyegrill.com
> 890 Seventh Avenue at 56th Street
> 212-541-9000
> Great for sushi, salads, sandwiches or fish.

253 Broadway at Warren Street
212-566-4621
> Mass transit
> N, R, J, M, Z - Canal Street

Manhattan Mall – 901 Avenue of Americas ar 32nd Street
212-279-8767
> Mass Transit
> B, D, F, N, Q, R, V, W - 34th Street

1700 Broadway - between 53rd & 54th Streets
212-307-5089
> Mass Transit
> #1 - 50th Street

Forest Hills, Queens
71-24 Austin Street at 71st Road
718 - 793-5491
> Mass transit
> Forest Hills - 71 Avenue - E, F, M, R
> 75th Avenue - E, F

Flushing, Queens
Fresh Meadows Shopping Center
61-18 188th Street - between Horace Harding Expressway
& 64th Avenue
718-264-2843

Bronx
Bay Plaza Shopping Center
352B Baychester Avenue at Bartow Avenue
(718) 862-0030

AMSTERDAM BOUTIQUE

Not the best quality, but lots of fun styles at low prices. If you accessorize it right, nobody will guess that the dress cost only $20. The clothes that they carry can either come off hookerish or if coordinated with panache look fabulous.

I bought a layered silk dress there that can be worn 12 different ways (they give you a direction sheet on how to tie it.) I've gotten many compliments on this dress and requests by friends to "pick me up one next time you're there."

Return policy
14 days with tags attached and receipt - store credit.
No returns after 14 days.

Manhattan
454 Broadway between Howard & Grand Streets
212-925-0422

For driving directions check http://www.mapquest.com
For discount parking check out http://www.bestparking.com and http://www.iconparking.com

>Mass transit
>J, M, Z, N, Q, R, W, 6 - Canal Street
>A, C, E - Canal Street - Church Street
>#1 - Canal - Varick Street

>Restaurant
>40 Carrots @ Bloomingdale's
>504 Broadway between Broome and Spring Streets
>See description on page 21.

MYSTIQUE
http://www.mystiqueboutiquenyc.com

When you feel the urge to be sexy, this is place to go. Filled with short slinky dresses, low cut cowl neck tops and skin tight leggings, Mystique will turn you into a siren in a flash and at a cut rate price. Their merchandise mix is trendy and young.

Return policy
No returns. Exchanges within 14 days.

LOCATIONS
For driving directions check http://www.mapquest.com
For discount parking check out http://www.bestparking.com and http://www.iconparking.com

Manhattan
324 Fifth Avenue between 32nd & 33rd Streets
917-351-0640

> Mass transit
> B, D, F, N, Q, R - 34th Street

547 Broadway between Spring & Prince Streets
212-274-0645

> Mass transit
> #4, 5, 6 - Spring Street
>
> Restaurant
> Lure
> 142 Mercer Street off Prince Street
> 212-431-7676
> See description on page 23.

368 Broadway Franklin & White Streets
212-349-8236

> Mass transit
> N, R - Canal Street
>
> Restaurant
> Sbarro
> 415 Broadway

212-334-7305
See description on page 26.

Manhasset, Long Island
1583 Northern Boulevard
516-441-5777

Melville, Long Island
925 Walt Whitman Road
631-923-0822

TOPSHOP
http://us.topshop.com/

The Sunday Times of London has written, "The High Street has never looked so haute." A British import that crossed the pond in 2009, Topshop has been a British fixture since 1964, providing up to the minute affordable fashion to UK fashionistas.

They carry everything from basics to the hottest cutting edge trends.

Return policy
30 days with receipt - full refund.
After 30 days or no receipt - exchange for the current selling price.

For driving directions check http://www.mapquest.com
For discount parking check out http://www.bestparking.com and http://www.iconparking.com

Manhattan
478 Broadway at Broome Street
212-966-9555

> Mass transit
> #6 - Spring Street
>
> Restaurant
> 40 Carrots @ Bloomingdale's
> 504 Broadway
> 212-729-5900

See description on page 21.

CONWAY STORES
http://www.conwaystores.com/

I was really hesitant about including Conway, a mass market merchandiser whose stores harken back to the ambiance of a 1910 lower east side pushcart, without the accompanying charm. Racks are positioned one on top of another, tightly packed and unorganized; items are strewn on the floor, walked and trampled on. There are long lines at checkout and sales help is nonexistent. Most of the items are in need of a good pressing. But, you can't beat the prices, usually less than $15. And if you have a fashion eye, you can discover some stylish items.

They have been in business for over 65 years and carry everything from women's, men's and children's clothing to shampoo, underwear, socks, jeans, tee shirts and toothpaste.

On occasion you can find some cute, if not particularly well made items. Shopping for summer is a better bet than for shopping for winter.

A few years ago I bought a denim summer dress that I wore incessantly. Really well styled and very comfortable.

But, be prepared for a less than stellar shopping experience. No dressing rooms. My advice if you're not local, is, buy it, find a nearby bathroom, try it on and then decide whether you will keep or return it.
Return policy
30 days with receipt - full refund or exchange.

LOCATIONS
For driving directions check http://www.mapquest.com
For discount parking check out http://www.bestparking.com and http://www.iconparking.com
Check their website for other locations throughout the city.

<u>Manhattan</u>
245 West 34th Street between Seventh & Eighth Avenues
212-868-0002

> <u>Mass transit</u>
> #1, 2, 3 - 34th Street - 7th Avenue

> <u>Restaurant</u>
> Sbarro
> 159 West 33rd Street at Seventh Avenue
> See description on page 26.

450 Seventh Avenue between 34th and 35th Streets
212- 967-1371

> <u>Mass transit</u>
> #1, 2, 3 - 34th Street - 7th Avenue

> <u>Restaurants</u>
> Sbarro
> 159 West 33rd Street at Seventh Avenue
> See description on page 26.

> Pret a Manger
> 485 Seventh Avenue at 36th Street
> 646-360-1625
> See description on page 19.

<u>Brooklyn</u>
427 Fulton Street
718-522-9200

> <u>Mass transit</u>
> #2, 3 - Fulton Mall

1633 East 16th Street
718-998-1046

> <u>Mass Transit</u>
> B, Q - Kings Highway

<u>Bronx</u>
215-223 East Fordham Road
718-563-1260

Mass transit
#4 - Fordham Road

Middle Village, Queens
66-26 Metropolitan Avenue
718-381.6771
Mass transit
F - 169th Street

Long Island City, Queens
34-37 48th Street
718-294-2102
Mass transit
G, R, V - 46th Street

KNOW STYLE

Cute, trendy items at low prices.
Return Policy
7 days credit with receipt and tags attached

Manhattan
80 Nassau Street at Fulton Street
212-227-7530
Mass transit
#2, 3, 4, 5, C, J, Z - Fulton Street

NECESSARY CLOTHING

http://www.necessaryclothing.com/
646-214-7881
Fun, young and inexpensive.

442 - 443 Broadway between Grand Street & Howard Street
Mass transit
#4, 6, 6X, J, N, Q, R, Z - Canal Street

676 Broadway
> Mass transit
> 4, 6 - Bleeker Street
> N, R - 8th Street

PRIMA DONNA

http://www.shopprimadonna.com

Their Manhattan store is located on Fifth Avenue, but don't let the location keep you away. Their prices will not break the bank. Sale shoes are priced at $10, $15 and $20. They carry clothing, accessories, jewelry and childrenswear.
Check their website for additional locations.
Return Policy
3 weeks for an exchange only
Sale items - final sale

Manhattan
433 Fifth Avenue between 38th & 39th Streets
212-481-4099
> Mass transit
> #7 - Fifth Avenue

Queens
71-24 Austin Street
Forest Hills
718-268-8069
> Mass transit
> E, F, M - 71 - Forest Hills

31-39 Steinway Street
Astoria
718-204-0488
> Mass transit
> E, M. R - Steinway Street

CHAPTER 3

DIRECT FROM THE SOURCE
You can get it for you wholesale

"We live not according to reason, but according to fashion."
Seneca - Roman philosopher, mid - 1st century AD

DIRECT FROM THE SOURCE
You can get it for you wholesale

Throughout the garment district (West 35th Street to 41st Street between Fifth and Eighth Avenues), intermingled with the fabric and trim stores are "wholesale only" stores that sell evening gowns, jackets, etc. Most are actually wholesale only and this is where some mom and pop boutiques buy their stock. But some of the stores are open to the public at wholesale prices.
All sales final.

For driving directions check http://www.mapquest.com
For discount parking check out http://www.bestparking.com and http://www.iconparking.com

DZHAVAEL COUTURE
http://www.dzhavael.com

Their collection is young, fashion forward and European inspired. Dresses start at $50.

Manhattan
247 West 37th Street between Seventh & Eighth Avenues
212-575-0454
Hours - 10:00 am - 7:00 pm
Closed Saturday.
> Mass transit
> #1, 7, N, Q - 34th Street

CHANTELLE FASHION LTD.
http://www.Chantellesale.com

They carry kicky clothing and furs (coats and sweaters) and have $25 and $39 racks.

Manhattan
46 West 37th Street
between Fifth Avenue & Avenue of the Americas
212-563-0488
Closed Saturday.
> Mass transit
> B, D, F, Q - 34th Street

ELI & COMPANY
http://www.accessoriescircle.com/manufacturers/eli-and-co-ny-inc/

They have a nice selection of handbags and accessories and some clothing.

Manhattan
207 West 37th Street Seventh & Eighth Avenues
212-398-2100
Closed Saturday.
> Mass transit
> #1, 7, N, Q - 34th Street

ALEXIS D
http://www.premisenyc.com

A selection of garments imported from France. Cash or credit.
Open Monday through Friday 9:00 am to 6:30 pm

Manhattan
240 West 37th Street
212-868-5510
> Mass transit
> #1, 7, N, Q - 34th Street

LILA MADISON//SHOWROOM OUTLET
www.missmadisonny.com

Inexpensive trendy dresses, gowns and sportswear.

<u>Manhattan</u>
556 Eighth Avenue at 37th Street
212-302-2472
> <u>Mass transit</u>
> #1, 7, N, Q - 34th Street
>
> <u>Restaurants</u>
> Pret a Manger
> 1410 Broadway at 39th Street
> Closed Sunday.
> See description on page 19.
>
> 530 Seventh Avenue
> Closed Saturday & Sunday.
>
> Café Metro
> 530 Seventh Avenue
> between 38th & 39thStreets
> 212-398-8788
> See description on page 20.

CHAPTER 4

SHOES
These boots are made for walking
(or maybe just for looking fabulous)

"About half my designs are controlled fantasy, 15 percent are total madness and the rest are bread-and-butter designs."
-Manolo Blanik

SHOES

These boots are made for walking
(or maybe just for looking fabulous)

Many women feel passionately about their shoes; note Carrie on "Sex and the City," who made Manolo's and Jimmy Choo's a religion. And speaking of Manolo, he designed a pair of shoes with five inch Lucite heels complete with flashing colored lights. The lights are activated when you walk, last 200 hours and can't be replaced when they burn out. The shoes cost $2500 and there's a waiting list for them!

Whether those boots were made for walking or just for looking fabulous, finding exceptionable shoes at a great price takes some fancy footwork. We all love a pair of FMPs and who doesn't look for shoes with toe cleavage? Here are a few stores that make the hunt easier. Also, try the resale shops, Century 21, TJ Maxx, Marshalls, Loehmann's and the other discounters listed in Chapter 1.

For driving directions check http://www.mapquest.com

MJM DESIGNER SHOES
http://mjmdesignershoes.com/index.shtml

MJM is a warehouse type store that discounts name brand shoes, carrying men's, women's and children's shoes; handbags and hosiery.

They have a section where items are further discounted and you can get some very good buys.
Return policy
30 days with receipt - full refund.
After 30 days - store credit at lowest selling price.

LOCATIONS
For driving directions check http://www.mapquest.com

East Meadow, Long Island
2501 Hempstead Turnpike

516-735-6111

<u>Glen Oaks, Long Island</u>
25801 Union Turnpike
516-328-0276

<u>Commack, Long Island</u>
210 Jericho Turnpike
631-864-5839

DSW
http://www.dsw.com/

Like MJM, DSW is a discounter of name brand shoes. They also carry a smattering of high end designers like, Taryn Rose and Marc Jacobs and a section where shoes are discounted 30% to 70%, the amount of the discount is indicated by a colored circle.

You can sign up for their frequent buyer card and accumulate points to be used for purchases.
<u>Return policy</u>
30 days with receipt - full refund.
After 30 days - gift card at current selling price.
Without receipt - gift card at current selling price.

LOCATIONS
For driving directions check http://www.mapquest.com
For discount parking check out http://www.bestparking.com and http://www.iconparking.com

<u>Manhattan</u>
40 East 14th Street off Fifth Avenue
212-674-2146

<u>Mass transit</u>
L - Sixth Avenue
F - 14th Street

Restaurant
Tocqueville
1 East 15th Street
212-647-1515
See description on page 23.

213 West 34th Street
212-967-9703

Mass transit
#1, 7, N, Q - 34th Street

Restaurants
Pret a Manger
485 Seventh Avenue
646-360-1625
See description on page 19.

Café Metro
530 Seventh Avenue at 38th Street
212-398-8788
See description on page 20.

2220 Broadway & 79th Street
917-746-9422

Mass transit
#1, 2 - 79th Street

Brooklyn
Atlantic Terminal
139 Flatbush Avenue
718-789-6973

Mass transit
B, M, N, R - Pacific Street

Elmhurst, Queens
Queens Place
88-01 Queens Boulevard
718-595-1361

Staten Island
2485 Richmond Avenue
718-477-1092

Carle Place, Long Island
357 Old Country Road
516-876-0204

Restaurant
Panera Bread
165 Old Country Road
Carle Place
516-739-2090
Sandwiches, all types of breads, salads.

Levittown, Long Island
Crescent Mall
3503 Hempstead Turnpike
516-520-1534

Syosset, Long Island
425 Jericho Turnpike
516-864-4630

Restaurants
Panera Bread
407 Jericho Turnpike
Syosset
516-677-5380

Sawa Sushi
260 Jericho Turnpike
Syosset
516-496-8886
See description on page 14.

Lawrence, Long Island
Bay Harbour Mall
345 Rockaway Turnpike
516-239-3018

<u>Huntington, Long Island</u>
1819 East Jericho Turnpike
631-858-9120

<u>Bronx</u>
Bay Plaza
2134 Bartow Ave
347-614-1490

"Whoever said money can't buy happiness simply didn't know where to go shopping."
~ Bo Derek

<u>CHAPTER 5</u>

BLING - NECK, EAR AND WRIST CANDY
Baubles, bangles & beads

FRAGRANCE
Scent of a woman (or man)

MAMA'S GOT A BRAND NEW BAG
(At these prices, mama's got two)

"I dress for the image. Not for myself, not for the public, not for fashion, not for men."
-Marlene Dietrich

BLING - NECK, EAR AND WRIST CANDY
Baubles, bangles & beads

FRAGRANCE
Scent of a woman (or man)

MAMA'S GOT A BRAND NEW BAG
(At these prices, mama's got two)

Have a hankering for some neck, ear, and wrist candy? Satisfy your cravings at the stores listed below. Sure 47th Street is known worldwide as the diamond district, but what about those of us who are just looking for some fun costume jewelry and don't want to spend a fortune? Lo-cal prices with hi-cal looks.

The stores are on Broadway between 28th and 32nd Streets. I've listed my favorites, but if you just walk up Broadway they line both sides of the street. A number of stores have also opened on West 28th Street between Broadway and Sixth Avenue. Those are also worth a look. Some of the stores on both Broadway and 28th Street are wholesale only, and they will post a sign to that effect. Others have a minimum purchase of between $20 and $100. The minimums vary from time to time so double check when you enter.

As of late there has been a turnover of these shops due to the fact that one block on Broadway between 29th and 30th Streets is being developed for, possibly a hotel.

The stores listed are where that trendy little boutique gets their stock. Uptown and in Soho, the same merchandise is double to ten times the price. In fact one of the shops I've listed sells their baubles to the boutiques in the major New York hotels.

Stick with me and I'll have you looking like you just strutted off the runway for less than $10. You may scoff now, but when you walk into these stores you'll be like a kid in a candy shop and the good part is, it is calorie free and you won't gain an ounce.

You will have to use your discriminating fashion eye and sift through the multitudes of baubles, bangles and bags to find the best pieces.

I've grouped the stores into one chapter as they're all in the same area. Most sell costume jewelry, but I've also included a source for handbags
and fragrances.

The merchandise is constantly changing and a store that had fabulous finds one week may not be the same one that has the best bling the next week. Repeated visits are called for

LOCATIONS
For driving directions check http://www.mapquest.com
For discount parking check out http://www.bestparking.com and http://www.iconparking.com

All locations listed below are in Manhattan.
> Mass transit
> N, B, D, F, Q, R W, V - 34th Street
> N, Q - 28th Street

BLING

JEWELRY IN TREND (formerly All About Trendz)
http://www.costumejewelry1.com/index.php/stores

This place is incredible!!!! You can walk out with a new wardrobe of chic jewelry for $25. Their merchandise will assault your senses and bedazzle your eyes.

When you walk in, they give you a small basket in which to put your selections. They do impose a $20 minimum (which any respectable fashionista will have no trouble meeting). Almost all of their stock is less than $10. Most items are in the $3 to $8 range. I can see you turning up your nose and hear you scoffing and saying, "what can you possibly get at that price?"

They carry a dizzying array of necklaces, bracelets, brooches, pashminas, earrings and jewelry sets (earrings and necklaces for $3 and $4). You may scoff now, but you will become an ardent devotee once you've shopped here.

One of my favorite finds here was a lizard brooch with multicolored stones. After my purchase, I was flipping through a Sotheby's Important Jewelry auction catalog and lo and behold, there was my brooch. I placed mine over the photo they pictured and it was exactly the same size down to the curve of the lizard's tail. Of course, the Sotheby's brooch used precious stones and mine, was not emeralds and rubies, but for $7.75, how can you go wrong?

1216 Broadway between 29th & 30th Streets
646-330-5977
59 West 31st Street
646-330-5767

U. S. JEWELRY HOUSE LTD.
This is a bit more upscale than All About Trendz. It's "members only", but it's free to join and all you need to join is a business card. They may also ask you for a resale number. Minimum purchase is $100.

When you walk in they ask for your membership card or number, give you a mini shopping cart and a small bottle of water. There are five long aisles chock full of all sorts of glittery, sparkling jewelry. Prices range from a few dollars to more than $150 for fabulous chunky beaded necklaces that would sell for three times that at a Madison Avenue boutique.
Warning - If you put something in your cart and decide at the register that it's not for you, they will charge you to restock it. So be sure to return anything you don't want to its rightful place before checking out.

1239 Broadway between 30th & 31st Streets
212-219-1272

EARRINGS PLAZA
They have the best prices on bracelets and a never ending selection. They also carry scarves, tiaras, cuff links, necklaces and brooches.

1263 Broadway between 31th & 32nd Streets
212-685-5666

JEWELRY HOUSE CORPORATION
42 West 28th Street between 6th Avenue & Broadway
212-689-7859
Closed on Sunday.

NIMA/N.A.I.
Bags, belts, jewelry, jewelry boxes, key chains. Their second floor showroom is chock full of goodies, however there is $100 minimum at the showroom and you must register (which isn't a big deal). However, you can buy a single piece at the storefront. They have a nice selection of small faux croc evening bags with rhinestone clasps that start at $21

The showroom usually has racks of belts, earrings and necklaces that are priced at $1. At my last visit they had an array of earrings at 4/$1.

1235 Broadway between 30th & 31st Streets
2nd floor
Storefront is right next door.
212-447-7472

PERLA DESIGNS
http://www.perlawholesale.com

Perla stocks a variety of jewelry and accessories. At the back of the store they have these adorable mini hats and headpieces ($5 and $6), perfect for a cocktail party or just for looking fabulous. They have a $50 minimum.

57 West 28th Street between Broadway & Avenue of the Americas
212-889-8085

NORLHA GIFT SHOP
http://www.norlhabeads.com

For a touch of the exotic, try Norlha Gift Shop. All items are made in Tibet, Nepal or India and have a boho ethnic look. The jewelry is crafted from resin, bone, horn, glass and turquoise.

They also carry handbags (evening clutches) and textiles. Norlha sells to museum shops who charge a premium, but you can snag a fabulous necklace for $12!

1179 Broadway between 27th & 28th Streets
646-415-8905

P & K JEWELRY
http://www.pandkjewelry.com/index.php

If you have the urge to splurge, sashay on down to P & K Jewelry. They are one of the world's largest sources for sterling silver and marcasite jewelry. They carry rings, earrings, necklaces, bracelets, pendants and pins and have some very upscale pieces that cost over $200 (these would retail at $600 to $800 at a Fifth Avenue store).

They also have wonderful $12 bracelets at the rear of the store. Any item marked net is 5% off, other items marked list are 65% off. Minimum purchase is $200.
Closed on Sunday.

1201 Broadway between 28th and 29th Streets
212-481-5658

HANDBAGS

DRANGO SPHERE INC.
http://www.drangpsphereny.con

It's in the bag. Bags, bags, and more bags. Drango has faux leather adaptations of the latest hot bags. They have a selection on the back wall by the register for $15. You need to use your style sense to sort through the good, bad and ugly.

151A West 30th Street
646-202-1618

FOREVER FASHION of NYC
http://picasaweb.google.com/foreverfashion109

A nice selection of handbags at bargain basement prices.

109 West 28th Street off Broadway
212-868-2988

FRAGRANCE

MANHATTAN WORLDWIDE INC.
Carries perfumes and colognes for men and women.

1200 Broadway between 29th & 30th Streets
212-696-0343

PERFUME DEPOT OF AMERICA INC.
Great prices on men's and women's fragrances.

1191 Broadway between 28th & 29th Streets
212-532-7515

Restaurants
Ayza Wine & Chocolate Bar
http://www.ayzanyc.com
11 West 31st Street (between Broadway and Fifth Avenue
212-714-2992

What could be a better combo than chocolate and wine? This charming bistro is right in the shopping hub of the Broadway area. Rest your weary body and feed your soul with fabulous chocolate confections that will jumpstart you. Or try their wonderful lunch/dinner selections (they have a weekday prix fixe lunch at $9.95) You can eat inside or out on the enclosed patio (heat lamps provide warmth if it's chilly). Try their chocolate martinis!

Fresh & Co.
http://www.freshandconyc.com
Seventh Avenue at West 30th Street
For a quick bite. Sandwiches, salads wraps, pastas, soups.

Pret a Manger
342 Seventh Avenue at 29th Street
See description on page 19.

CHAPTER 6

HATS - HEAD TRIP
In your Easter bonnet . . .

"I enjoy hats. And when one has filthy hair, that is a good accessory."
-Julia Roberts

HATS - HEAD TRIP
In your Easter bonnet . . .

Back in the 1930s, '40s and '50s no fashionable woman would have been caught dead leaving the house without a hat. Flirty cocktail hats with peek-a-boo veiling, ferocious fedoras, head hugging cloches and jaunty chapeaux abounded. The millinery industry thrived. The 1960s brought a more casual bent to fashion and hats fell from favor and off of women's heads.

Personally, I love hats (this may be due to the fact that my grandfather was a milliner and it's in my blood). I have a collection of both current and vintage hats and a bunch of cocktail hats that I've designed and made. I wear a hat every chance I get. I've found that people perceive you differently when you don a chapeau. I'm not talking a baseball hat, but a proper wide brim straw hat perfect for sunning at that party in the Hampton's or a British Bowler (like the one Steed wore in "The Avengers") or even a charming 1930s cocktail hat with a bunch of cherries trimming it that could have been worn at the El Morocco. Hats express your personality in the same manner that clothing does.

The British know how to do hats. Note those "fascinators" worn with such aplomb at Kate and William's royal wedding. Though Phillip Treacy's creation wasn't everyone's cup of Earl Grey tea, the topper worn by Princess Beatrice fetched over $130,000 at auction for UNICEF UK and Children in Crisis, Princess Beatrice's Little Bee Initiative.

Unfortunately, the millinery district in New York has all but disappeared. It used to be located between Fifth Avenue and Avenue of the Americas on 38th Street. But, for those who have a yen for a chapeau I've listed the few hat emporiums that are still operating.

Mass transit
B, D, F, Q - 42nd Street

MANNY'S MILLINERY SUPPLY

http://www.mannys-millinery.com/

Manny's has been in business for more than 60 years, since the era of Dior's New Look. They carry hats in a wide variety of straws and fur felts, beavers and suedes, in addition to buckram frames. Trims including flowers, feathers, ribbons, veiling and braids. One of the few old time millinery resources. Want a fabulous hat for Ascot? An Easter bonnet that will turn heads on Fifth Avenue? They've got it or you can design it.
Hours
Monday-Thursday - 10:00 - 5:30

Manhattan
28 West 38th Street
between Fifth Avenue & Avenue of the Americas
212-840-2235

HAT CESSORY

I dubbed this place "Hallelujah - The Source for Serious Hats to Wear to Church or Synagogue."

They start at $10 for an unadorned hat that is available in a rainbow of colors. Prices escalate depending on what trims you select. It's like build a bear for adults. Unleash the designer that lurks inside of you and create your own fashion fabulous head topper.

Manhattan
60 West 38th Street
between Fifth Avenue & Avenue of the Americas
212-302-3934

> Restaurant
> Pret a Manger
> 1020 Avenue of the Americas at 38th Street
> 646-688-1061
> Open 7 days.
> See description on page 19.

<u>NOTES</u>

"Shopping is better than sex. If you're not satisfied after shopping you can make an exchange for something you really like."

~ Adrienne Gusoff

<u>CHAPTER 7</u>

DIAMONDS + GIRLS
= BFF
"Square cut or pear shaped,
these rocks don't lose their shape"

"Better a diamond with a flaw than a pebble without."
Confucius

"Kissing your hand may make you feel very very good
but a diamond and sapphire bracelet lasts forever."
Anita Loos - Hollywood Screenwriter and Novelist

DIAMONDS + GIRLS = BFF

"Square cut or pear shaped,
these rocks don't lose their shape"

THE DIAMOND DISTRICT - 47TH STREET
http://www.diamonddistrict.org/
West 47th Street between 5th Avenue & Avenue of the Americas
212-302-5739

Forty-seventh Street is known worldwide as the Diamond District. From Fifth Avenue to Avenue of the Americas, the street is filled with jewelry merchants, selling fine jewelry, gold, pearls, diamonds and other precious stones, all competing for your business.

You can find watches, antique and estate jewelry and lots of places that do jewelry repair, watch repair, engraving, pearl re-stringing and stone setting.

Check out the Diamond District website for a glossary of terms, shopping tips and suggestions on what to know before buying. Shop around to find the best deal and remember the advice of Marilyn Monroe in "Gentlemen Prefer Blondes."
"A kiss on the cheek may be quite continental, but diamonds are a girl's best friend."

> Mass transit
> B, D, F, V - 47th - 50th Street - Rockefeller Center
> For driving directions check http://www.mapquest.com
> For discount parking check out http://www.bestparking.com
> and http://www.iconparking.com

FINE JEWELRY & DIAMONDS OFF CANAL STREET
Nestled between Little Italy and Chinatown, near Canal Street is another source for diamonds and fine gold jewelry.

All real, no faux. A mini-version of 47th Street.
> Mass transit
> N, R - Canal Street

STARLIGHT JEWELRY COMPANY

I've dealt with Sue and John, the owners and they're terrific.

80 Bowery off Canal Street
212-219-8764

NOTES

"If men liked shopping, they'd call it research."
~ Cynthia Nelms

CHAPTER 8

HERE COMES THE BRIDE

A PRINCESS BRIDE
Crown her

"Fashions fade, style is eternal."
-Yves Saint Laurent

HERE COMES THE BRIDE

Years ago you could go into one of the so-called "bridal buildings" (they were grouped primarily in one or two buildings on Seventh Avenue or Broadway) on a Saturday and ask the elevator starter who was selling bridal gowns wholesale. That's not the case anymore. But a savvy bride can still find the perfect dress at a great price. Any saving on the dress can be used to offset your catering costs and maybe then you can afford to invite your great-aunt Phoebe (after all, she is known to give a generous gift).

Also, check with the gown company of the dress of your dreams to see if they have a sample sale. Many do. And remember, "you don't alter Vera Wang to fit you, you alter you to fit Vera Wang."

THE BRIDAL GARDEN
http://www.bridalgarden.org

The Bridal Garden opened in 1998, as a fundraising arm for Sheltering Arms Children's Service.

This nonprofit boutique offers designer gowns at up to 75 percent off retail. Designers, and boutiques donate samples and brand-new gowns from names like Ulla-Maija, Angel Sanchez, and Vera Wang and proceeds from the reduced price sales benefit the charity. They also sell consumer donated couture and designer gowns. They have a huge selection of gowns and veils organized by style. Alterations are not included in the price.

This is not a large space, but it's very well organized.
By appointment only.

LOCATION
For driving directions check http://www.mapquest.com
For discount parking check out http://www.bestparking.com and http://www.iconparking.com

Manhattan
54 West 21st Street - Ste. 907 near Avenue of the Americas

212-252-0661

Mass transit
N, R, - 23rd Street.& Broadway
F, V - 23rd Street & 6th Avenue
#1, 9 - 23rd Street & 7th Avenue

Restaurant
Tocqueville
1 East 15th Street
212-647-1515
This elegant restaurant is just the place to go for a lady's lunch after shopping for a wedding gown. They have a $29.00 three course prix fixe lunch that is just wonderful.

KLEINFELD
http://www.facebook.com/event.php?eid=269373969542&index=1

This is the "Say Yes to the Dress" store. They have a huge inventory that they regularly cull at their "Blow Out" sales and their sample sales. Sample sales are held every month and you must call for a one hour appointment. "Blow Out" sales are held every three months. Line up with friends and family and grab whatever you can. Then barter and trade with other brides-to-be. First come, first served, cash/check/credit card and carry. Check their Facebook page for dates.

110 West 20th Street
646-633-4300

Mass transit
23rd Street (PATH)
F, V - 23rd Street - 6th Avenue
#1 - 18th Street - 7th Avenue
For driving directions check http://www.mapquest.com
For discount parking check out http://www.bestparking.com
and http://www.iconparking.com

Restaurant
Tocqueville
See description on page 63.

MICHAEL'S - THE CONSIGNMENT SHOP FOR WOMEN
http://www.michaelsconsignment.com

In addition to their regular inventory, Michael's has a very nice selection of designer wedding gowns. Prices range from $800 to $3,000, with most running around $1,200 - $1,500. Compared to the prices on their typical inventory the gowns are a bargain. I've spotted Vera Wang, Badgley Mischka, Amsale, Reem Acra and Kenneth Pool on the racks. Their stock is constantly updated, so if at first you don't succeed...

Manhattan
1041 Madison Avenue between 79th & 80th Streets
(upstairs)
212-737-7273
> Mass transit
> #6 - 77th Street
> For driving directions check http://www.mapquest.com
> For discount parking check out http://www.bestparking.com or http://iconparking.com
>
> Restaurant
> Atlantic Grill
> 1341 Third Avenue at 77th Street
> 212-988-9200
> http://www.brguestrestaurants.com/restaurants/atlantic_grill/index.php
> Terrific for lunch with both indoor and outdoor seating. I love their crab cake sandwiches! They often offer a three course $25.00 prix fixe menu at lunch.

RK BRIDAL
http://www.rkbridal.com

RK has a very large selection of gowns from mid-price companies, Alfred Angelo, Allure, St. Patrick, La Sposa, Mori Lee, etc. Their prices range from $500 to $3500. They also carry bridesmaids' gowns, flower girl dresses, veils, shoes and jewelry. On weekends, brides start lining up in the lobby at 9:00 a.m.. Go during the week for a ore more civilized shopping experience.

Manhattan
318 West 39th Street between Eighth & Ninth Avenues
212-947-1155
Open 7 days from 11:00 a.m.
Saturday from 9:30 a.m.

Mass transit
#1 - Times Square - 42nd Street
#2, 3, 7, A, C, E, S, N, Q, R, W - 7th Avenue & 42nd Street
#7, B, D, F, V - 42nd Street - 5th Avenue - 6th Avenue

A PRINCESS BRIDE
Crown her

DESIGN BY NOVA
This store carries an array of tiaras. Those from China start at $21; Swarovski crystal encrusted crowns start at $96. These prices are almost always 50% off.
Return policy
All sales final.

Manhattan
1000 Avenue of the Americas between 37th & 38th Streets
212-719-2744

Mass transit
#1 - Times Square - 42nd Street
#2, 3, 7, A, C, E, S, N, Q, R, W - 7th Avenue & 42nd Street
#7, B, D, F, V - 42nd Street - 5th Avenue - 6th Avenue
PATH - 33rd Street

Restaurant
Pret a Manger
1020 Avenue of the Americas - 38th Street
Open 7 days.
See description on page 19.

SHINETRIM
http://www.shinetrim.com

Tiaras, combs, veils, bridal accouterments.
Open Monday - Saturday.

Manhattan
228 West 39th Street - 2nd floor
212-869-8887

> Mass transit
> #1 - Times Square - 42nd Street
> #2, 3, 7, A, C, E, S, N, Q, R, W - 7th Avenue & 42nd Street
> #7, B, D, F, V - 42nd Street - 5th Avenue - 6th Avenue
> PATH - 33rd Street

CHAPTER 9

CONSIGNMENT SHOPS
What goes around comes around

"The difference between style and fashion is quality."
-Giorgio Armani

CONSIGNMENT SHOPS
What goes around comes around

There is a plethora of consignment shops on the upper east side, possibly due to density of high quality consigners that inhabit the area. This makes for stock that is constantly refreshed. You can hit them all in one day and then go for lunch or brunch.

If the stars are in alignment and mercury is not in retrograde, you can snare a runway treasure at a street smart price.

MICHAEL'S - THE CONSIGNMENT SHOP FOR WOMEN
http://www.michaelsconsignment.com

Michael's is one of the original consignment shops on the upper east side. They have all the top designers and carry clothing, shoes, bags and jewelry. Nicely laid out on two floors. I find that their prices are a bit high, but if you have to have that Chanel jacket, $750 is much better than $3000. Their stock is current and in excellent condition.
Return Policy
All sales final.

Manhattan
1041 Madison Avenue between 79th & 80th Streets
(upstairs)
212-737-7273

> Mass transit
> #6 - 77th Street
> For driving directions check http://www.mapquest.com
> For discount parking check out http://www.bestparking.com
> and http://www.iconparking.com
>
> Restaurant
> Atlantic Grill
> 1341 Third Avenue at 77th Street
> 212-988-9200
> See description on page 64.

ENCORE - THE PREMIER CONSIGNMENT SHOP
http://www.encoreresale.com/

Encore, established in 1954, was one of the first designer consignment shops in the United States. The Grande Dame of New York's retail consignment shops, they specialize in new or almost new, couture/designer clothing and accessories. They are open seven days a week (but are closed on Sunday in January).

They are upstairs, their prices are good and they also have an eBay store.
Return Policy
All sales final.

Manhattan
1132 Madison Avenue between 84th & 85th Streets
2nd & 3rd floors
212-879-2850
>Mass transit
>#4, 5, 6, - 86th Street
>For driving directions check http://www.mapquest.com
>For discount parking check out http://www.bestparking.com
>and http://www.iconparking.com

BIS DESIGNER RESALE
http://www.bisbiz.com/

Next door to Encore, also one flight up; ring the bell and they will buzz you in. Bis is another source for designer/couture clothing and accessories at very good prices and they also have an eBay store.
Return Policy
All sales final.

Manhattan
1134 Madison Avenue between 84th & 85th Streets
212-396-2760
>Mass transit
>#4, 5, 6 - 86th Street
>For driving directions check http://www.mapquest.com

For discount parking check out http://www.bestparking.com
and http://www.iconparking.com

DESIGNER RESALE & GENTLEMEN'S RESALE
http://www.designerresaleconsignment.com

Housed in three street level brownstones, this elegant shop is
beautifully laid out. It almost feels as if you're in a private home.
Rooms meander from one to another; floors are highly polished wood
and merchandise is a diverse designer mix. They indicate 20% or
50% off by the color of the tag.

For the man in your life they have a men's consignment shop right
next door.
Return Policy
All sales final.

Manhattan
324 & 322 East 81st Street between Second & Third Avenues
212-734-3639
> Mass transit
> #6 - 77th Street
> For driving directions check http://www.mapquest.com
> For discount parking check out http://www.bestparking.com
> and http://www.iconparking.com
>
> Restaurant
> Atlantic Grill
> 1341 Third Avenue at 77th Street
> See description on page 64.

LA BOUTIQUE RESALE
http://www.laboutiqueresale.com

They have three locations on the Upper East Side. A nice selection
of designer merchandise at very fair prices.
Return Policy
All sales final.

For driving directions check http://www.mapquest.com
For discount parking check out http://www.bestparking.com and http://www.iconparking.com

LOCATIONS
Manhattan
1045 Madison Avenue near 80th Street
212-517-8099
Open 7 days.

> Mass transit
> #6 - 77th Street

> Restaurant
> Atlantic Grill
> 1341 Third Avenue at 77th Street
> See description on page 64.

141 East 62nd Street - 2nd floor corner of Lexington Avenue
212-588-8898
Closed Sunday.

> Mass transit
> #4, 5, 6 -59th Street
> B, Q - Lexington Avenue

> Restaurant
> Serendipity 3
> http:www.serendipity3.com
> 225 East. 60th Street off Third Avenue
> 212-838-3531
> Be a kid again and satisfy your sweet tooth with an ice cream soda or hot chocolate. A New York landmark, they define themselves as "the art of making happy discoveries or finding the unexpectedly pleasant by chance . . . " For the unexpected try their frozen hot chocolate. Frequented by the rich and famous, you may run into former President Clinton. I know it's a calorie nightmare, but don't you deserve a treat once in a while? Be prepared for a long wait for a table.

SECOND TIME AROUND
http://www.secondtimearound.net

Second Time Around is an upscale consignment company that carries new and almost-new designer clothing and accessories. The original store, outside of Boston was opened in 1973 by Dottie Casler. They now have 24 stores in ten states .

They carry a great mix of designer clothing and accessories at reasonable prices.

94 7th Avenue between 15th and 16th Streets
212-255-9455

Mass transit
#1, 2, 3, A, C, E, F, M, L - Union Square

1040 Lexington Avenue between 74th & 75th Streets
212-628-0980

Mass transit
#6 - 77th Street

Restaurant
Vivolo
http://www.vivolonyc.com
140 East 74th Street
212-737-3533
Housed on two floors of a townhouse, Vivolo is an elegant place for lunch or dinner serving wonderful Italian specialties.

111 Thompson Street
212-925-3919

Mass transit
A - Spring Street

2624 Broadway at 99th Street
212-666-3500

Mass transit
#1 - 103rd Street
#1, 2, 3 - 96th Street
A, B, C - 96th Street

262 Mott Street

212-965-8415

> Mass transit
> # 6 - Bleecker Street

232 Third Avenue between 19th and 20th Streets

212-228-8879

> Mass transit
> #4, 6, 6X - 23rd Street

238 West 72nd Street

212-362-6226

> Mass transit
> #1, 2, 3 - 72nd Street

Forest Hills, Queens
70-49 Austin Street

718-575-8805

> Mass transit
> E, F, M, R - Forest Hills - 71st Avenue
> E, F - 75th Avenue

Huntington, Long Island
276 Main Street

631-351-4070

WORTH THE TRIP

There are four resale shops located in Nassau County on the North Shore of Long Island and one in Sag Harbor on the east end of the Island that are worth checking out.

For driving directions check http://www.mapquest.com

NEXT TO NEW

This is a bit of a shlep from the city, but their prices are great. (I heard a woman say that she comes all the way from New Jersey to shop here.)

Next To New carries mostly bridge lines, but occasionally you can stumble upon a designer gem.

I've picked up a black and white wool tweed Chanel jacket for $125 and a pair of Chanel mules for $35. But, that is rare. I did recently find Jimmy Choo's, Manolo's and Chanel mules all priced less than $80. They discount by 50% anything that has been there more than 21 to 30 days. This is indicated by the color of the tag and they post these at the register. Anything over 60 days is given to charity. Their stock is current and the racks are organized by color. They carry clothing, shoes, jewelry, belts, and bags.

Return Policy

All sales final.

Oyster Bay, Long Island
59 West Main Street
Oyster Bay
516-922-3636

> Mass transit
> LIRR to Oyster Bay (the last stop) 75 minutes from Penn Station. The shop is a five minute walk from the train.

> Restaurants
> Both within walking distance and very good.

> Wild Honey
> http://www.wildhoneyrestaurant.com
> 1 East Main Street - Oyster Bay
> 516-922-4690

> Jack Halyards
> http://www.jackhalyardstavern.com
> 62 South Street - Oyster Bay
> 516-922-2999

WORTH REPEATING

Betsy runs this Locust Valley resale shop that is chock full of clothing and accessories. The racks are really packed. She often has a discount rack with items for $5, $10, $15. She carries more designer items than Next To New and therefore her prices are bit higher.

Twice a year (in March and in late August or September) she holds a $5 Blow-Out sale where a myriad of items are only $5. At the last sale, I uncovered a white Battenburg lace skirt by Calypso, a printed silk Calypso shirt and a halter top with a huge jeweled piece on the front.

Return Policy
All sales final.

Hours - Tuesday - 2:00 pm - 7:00 pm
Wednesday - Saturday - 11:00 am - 6:00 pm
Sunday - 12 noon - 4:00 pm

Locust Valley, Long Island
83 Birch Hill Road
Locust Valley
516-759-5726

ONE LAST LOOK

https://www.facebook.com/pages/One-Last-Look-Consignment-Bout
ique/578829522166186?fref=ts

A charming boutique filled with designer and contemporary labels. Christina, the owner will help you put together the perfect outfit. Their motto is, "style is always in fashion, red carpet service is never out of vogue and the customer is always #1."

Consignees receive a 50/50 split. Items are marked down 20% after 60 days.

Return Policy
All sales final

Locust Valley, Long Island
37 Forest Avenue
516-399-2600
Mass transit
LIRR to Locust Valley (the Oyster Bay line) about 65 minutes from Penn Station. The shop is a five minute walk from the train.

Restaurant
Buckram's Stables Cafe
31 Forest Avenue
516-671-3080

REVIVAL
http://www.revivalboutique.com

Packed to the rafters with both current and vintage designer items,
Revival has both couture pieces and designer RTW. You can find a
large assortment of handbags (LV, Chanel, Hermes, Prada, etc.) and
shoes (Choo, Manolo, Louboutin) alongside cases of jewelry and
vintage beaded handbags. Their prices are not inexpensive, but if you
yearn for that special designer item at a less than retail cost, you can
probably find it at Revival.
Return Policy
All sales final

Roslyn, Long Island
1374 Old Northern Boulevard
516-299-4556

Restaurants
Diane's Trattoria
21 Bryant Avenue - Roslyn
516- 621-2591

Diane's Bakery
23 Bryant Avenue - Roslyn
516- 621-2522
A great place for a sugar high and a cup of java.

MP Taverna
http://www.mptaverna.com
1363 Old Northern Boulevard - Roslyn
516-686-6486
This beautifully appointed Greek inspired restaurant has a
varied menu and a $15 three course prix fixe lunch.

Bistro Citron
1362 Old Northern Boulevard
516-403-4400
A charming place for a ladies' lunch overlooking a pond.
Crepes, sandwiches, mussels, salads.

CORNER CLOSET

If you're out on the East End of Long Island stop into Corner Closet.
It's nestled in the hamlet of Sag Harbor and not far from East
Hampton. Owner, Seena Stromberg, a veteran fashion industry
manufacturer opened the shop in February 2011. Corner Closet
carries fabulous high end women's and men's designer items of
pristine quality, all authentic. A great selection of Chanel handbags,
Pucci, Hermes and other top designers. It's hard to believe that
they're pre-owned.

Return Policy
All sales final

Open 7 days a week
Monday - Thursday - 10 to 7
Friday - Sunday - 10 to 8.
If you are looking for something specific you can email her at
thecornercloset@aol.com

Sag Harbor, Long Island
108 Main Street
631-808-3005

Restaurants
Page
63 Main Street, Sag Harbor
631-725-1810
Page offers a diverse menu of salads, sandwiches and "on
the half shell" selections served in a charming brick walled
and tin ceilinged room. Wonderful crab cakes and lobster
BLT's.

Golden Pear Cafe
http://www.goldenpearcafe.com/index.htm

111 Main Street, Sag Harbor
631-725-2270
For a quick tasty lunch of salads, wraps and sandwiches or
hot dishes, try Gold Pear Café.

COLLETTE

http://colletteconsignment.com/southampton/
Collette has been offering designer items at discounted prices for over
fourteen years.   Everything from Hermes Birkin bags to red soled
Louboutin shoes, couture and a whole lot of Chanel. Their prices run
the gamut but you can find real gems at their basement or tent sales.
I spotted a fabulous pair of Manolo sandals for $38.   Unfortunately
they were a bit too small.
Return Policy
All sales final

Southampton, Long Island
10 Main Street - Collette's Basement
22 Main Street
631-287-1867

Restaurant
75 Main Street
http://www.75main.com/brunch-menu
A diverse menu and they serve a great brunch all day until
4:00 pm.

CHAPTER 10

VINTAGE
Everything old is new again

"If the shoe fits, buy it in every color."

VINTAGE
Everything old is new again

Vintage denotes anything that was produced between the 1920s and the 1980s. Items before 1920 are considered antique.

Vintage and antique clothing and accessories can be found in thrift stores, charity shops, estate sales and stores solely devoted to this genre. Ebay (http://www.ebay.com) and Etsy (http://www.etsy.com) can also be a source for discovering vintage gems.

I've regularly uncovered vintage handbags (from the 40s and 50s) at estate sales for between $5 and $10. My last big score was at a garage sale that I stopped at, at 1:00 pm. (I'm not a crack of dawn shopper). The man running it was selling his father's office equipment but had a table filled with handbags; the price $1 each. I scored a vintage 1940s bag, a bronze beaded bag from the 1920s and a leather faux Chanel.

I tend to gravitate to clothing and accessories prior to the 1960s. I have a collection of both antique and vintage clothing ranging from the 1870s through the 1980s.

Wearing antique or vintage garments can be challenging. You have to be cognizant of the fact that some garments may come off looking like a costume. You don't want to look as if you came off of the set of "Gone With The Wind". I own a gorgeous white cotton tea dress from 1910 but have yet to wear it. However, a blouse from the same era works with a pair of jeans. And, though "everything old is new again" when it comes around again, it usually has a different twist.

Antique clothing (prior to the 1920s) tends to run small as people were smaller, especially in the waist area. In addition, many older garments don't have size, fiber content or care labels.

The real perk of wearing vintage is that it is usually one of a kind and you won't see yourself coming and going in it. In an era of mass production (even in designer clothing), you can be truly unique.

Many shops that claim to carry vintage, don't. They may have one or

two items but are not vintage stores. I've visited quite a few in preparing this chapter and have only included the stores that sell primarily vintage clothing and accessories. I've also found that they tend to be a bit on the expensive side. Be aware that shopping at stores carrying vintage clothing and accessories will not be inexpensive. It is not a discount shopping experience. If you want to look like Audrey Hepburn in "Breakfast At Tiffany's" it will cost you.
If you crave that unique, one of a kind look be prepared to pay for it.

Tips for Buying Vintage

1.   Look for quality fabrics. If it's made from a quality fabric, it's usually a better garment. Look for natural fibers-wool, linen, silk, cotton, ramie. Rayon tends to pill (those nasty little fuzz balls). Any garment prior to the 1930s will be made from a natural fiber as synthetics didn't hit the market until the 30s. Rayon was the first on the scene. They tried to create a man made copy of silk. In fact, the original name of rayon was "artificial silk". Not a good marketing ploy.
2.   Look for designer labels.
3.   Don't get discouraged if on your first or even second trip you leave empty-handed. It takes persistence.
4.   If the shop smells funky; give it a pass.
5.   Check for imperfections, stains, rips, etc. Some can be fixed, some not. What will it cost to clean the item? I bought a Chanel jacket at a thrift sale with some spots on the front. The jacket was $25, so I took a chance and had it cleaned. The stains came out
      Underarm perspiration stains won't come out and additionally they degrade the fabric, especially silk.
6.   Make sure it fits. It's not a deal if it will cost you $25-$100 in alterations.

VINTAGE CLOTHING & ANTIQUE TEXTILE
SHOW & SALE
http://www.manhattanvintage.com
Check their website for scheduled shows in the Fall and Spring.

This show groups 90 top vintage clothing dealers under one roof.

Admission is $20. The website offers a discount coupon.

MARMALADE VINTAGE
http://www.marmaladevintage.com

Relocated from her Ludlow Street store, Hannah Kurland stocks
pristine clothing and accessories by 1970s and 1980s designers such
as Maude Frizon, Norma Kamali, Issey Miyake, Koos Van den Akker
and Claude Montana.
Open from 1:00 pm to 7:00 pm everyday

174 Mott Street at Broome Street
212-473-0870
>Mass transit
>#6 - Spring Street

STELLA DALLAS
Packed with a selection of vintage clothing and accessories, mostly
spanning the 1950s through the 1980s, Stella Dallas is a fun place to
shop. Lots of Western boots and peasant blouses.

218 Thompson Street
212-674-0447
>Mass Transit
>B, D, F, M - Broadway - Lafayette Street
>A, C, E - Spring Street
>#4. 6 - Bleeker Street

Williamsburg, Brooklyn
10 FT SINGLE BY STELLA DALLAS
10 Ft. Single is a loft-sized vintage clothing store that carries a large
selection of vintage clothing for both men and women. The store is
divided into two rooms; one carrying 80s-90s vintage and the other
room stocks more expensive items from the 40s through the 70s.

285 N. 6th Street (near Metropolitan Avenue)
718-486-9482

<u>Mass Transit</u>
G - Metropolitan Avenue
L - Lorimer Street; Bedford Avenue

<u>Manhattan</u>
The two shops listed below are on Rivington Street, an area that at the turn of the 20th century housed Jewish immigrants in tenements, some of which still stand.

<u>Mass Transit</u> .
F - Delancey Street or 2nd Avenue
J, M, Z - Essex Street

EDITH MACHINIST
http://www.edithmachinist.com

A large selection of handbags and shoes, as well as clothing.

104 Rivington Street (off Ludlow Street)
212-979-9992

NARNIA
http://www.narniavintage.com

A profusion of printed and patterned clothing greets you at Narnia. Very Boho-California chic with clothing from the 1960s through 80s.

161 Rivington Street between Clinton and Suffolk
212-979-0661

SYLVIA PINES UNIQUITIES
Sylvia has been in business at this location for 35 years. Her shop has a fabulous selection of antique and vintage handbags dating from the Victorian era through the 1940s. Gorgeous handbags - beaded, petit point and crocheted creations, the majority of which have been created by hand. Where in today's market can you find that? With

mass produced designer bags costing thousands of dollars, a bag from Uniquities is a fraction of that price and each is unique.
Tue-Sat 9:30 am - 5 pm

1102 Lexington Avenue at 77th Street

212-744-5141

Mass Transit
4, 6, 6X - 77th Street or Hunter College - 68th Street

Restaurants
Atlantic Grill
1341 Third Avenue at 77th Street
212-988-9200
See description on page 64.

Vivolo
http://www.vivolonyc.com
140 East 74th Street off Lexington Avenue
212-737-3533
See description on page 72.

Huntington, Long Island
LOTUS VINTAGE
www.lotusvintage.com/
http://www.etsy.com/shop/LotusvintageNY

Lotus Vintage has both an online and a brick and mortar store. You'll find an eclectic mix of clothing spanning the 50s through the 90s. Adrian specializes in boho fashions of the 60s and 70s but also has classic 50s styles. Her prices are reasonable. I've seen similar items at a vintage shop in Manhattan at four times the price.

12 West Carver Street
631-470-7795

CHAPTER 11

THRIFT SHOPS
The thrill of the hunt

"I don't do fashion, I am fashion."
-Coco Chanel

THRIFT SHOPS
The thrill of the hunt

Like consignment shops, but more so, thrift shops are hit or miss. Many buy their stock by the pound (from those donate clothing bins situated throughout the area). They then go through the items, discard what's really nasty or put what is worth more than a thrift shop price on eBay and then sell the remainder at their shop. The quality of the stock and pricing will depend on who is doing the ticketing and how much they know about fashion. It's unlikely that you'll find a Gucci or Prada dress, but lesser known lines that don't get the press, often turn up. As a fashionista, you, of course, are up on the hottest fashion labels. As with the consignment shops, you have to be diligent and shop often. Thrift shops are the perfect place to find a gem and add another notch to your discount shopping belt.

Check out your local church, synagogue or senior center. Many have thrift shops.

Thrift shops generally do not accept returns.

BEACON'S CLOSET
http://www.beaconscloset.com
Beacon's Closet is a buy, sell or trade shop. The Williamsburg store is HUGE, 5500 square feet, set up by color and has a vast selection of both designer, vintage and current merchandise; men's and women's clothing, shoes, bags, accessories, even CD's. I've spotted a silk charmeuse Marchesa top for $25, Helmut Lang, Betsey Johnson (with the tags still on) alongside vintage 70s and 80s items and H&M and Banana Republic. I've picked up an Alexander McQueen strapless summer dress with a triple wrap belt for $18 (though it was his Target line) it fit like a glove and was made beautifully. The salesperson kept saying she didn't know how she missed scooping this up. A friend of mine found a Chanel wool winter coat for $99

As stated, the space is humongous, so give yourself plenty of time to peruse. Word of this second-hand shop has spread far and wide so don't be surprised if you hear French, Russian and Japanese spoken

It attracts hip, twenty to thirty-somethings searching for artsy duds.

You can also shop online at their website. They offer free domestic shipping.

If you would like to sell them your treasures, their policy for buying is as follows: They pay you on the spot; 35% cash, or 50% store credit, based on the price put on the item. No appointment necessary. They ask that you bring no more than four bags.

Return Policy
All sales final

Williamsburg, Brooklyn
88 N 11th Street - between Berry and Wythe
718-486-0816
Monday -Friday - 11a.m. - 9 p.m.
Saturday and Sunday -11a.m. - 8 p.m.

> Mass transit
> L train - Bedford Avenue.
> Walk up Bedford Avenue in the direction of traffic for 4 blocks to N. 11th Street. Make a left on N 11th Street. walk up N 11th Street for 1 and a half blocks, past Berry, to #88. The shop is across from the Brooklyn Brewery.

> Restaurant
> Fabiane's
> http://www.fabianescafeandpastry.com/
> 142 N 5th Street at Bedford Avenue
> 718-218-9632
> See description on page 18.

Park Slope, Brooklyn
92 5th Avenue at Warren Street
718-230-1630
Monday - Friday Noon-9p.m.
Saturday and Sunday -11a.m. - 8 p.m.

> Mass transit
> B, D, N, Q - Atlantic/Pacific
> #2, #3 - Bergen Street - walk to 5th Ave & head south.

Manhattan
10 W 13th Street (between Fifth Avenue & Avenue of the Americas)
(917) 261-4863
<u>Mass transit</u>
#4, 5, 6, L, N, R - Union Square

BUFFALO EXCHANGE
http://www.buffaloexchange.com

Buffalo Exchange straddles the line between thrift and consignment. A happy marriage of the two.

The first Buffalo Exchange was opened in 1974 in Tucson, Arizona by a Swedish woman. The concept, like Beacon's Clsoet, is buy, sell or trade. Customers bring in items to trade for cash on the spot! Or you can just shop their store. They carry both pre-owned and new merchandise that changes constantly. Men's and women's clothing and accessories. They currently have 37 stores in 14 states. They stock mostly basic clothing; t-shirts, jeans and the like.

LOCATIONS
Manhattan
332 East 11th Street between First & Second Avenues
212-260-9340
<u>Mass transit</u>
L - 1st Avenue

114 West 26th Street
212-675-3535
<u>Mass transit</u>
#1, 2, N, R - 28th Street

Williamsburg, Brooklyn
504 Driggs Avenue
N. 9th Street
718-384-6901
<u>Mass transit</u>
L - Bedford Avenue
For driving directions check http://www.mapquest.com

For discount parking check out http://www.bestparking.com and http://www.iconparking.com

THE ARTHRITIS THRIFT SHOP

In addition to men's and women's clothing and accessories, they carry a bit of furniture and bric-a-brac. The racks are jammed full and aren't organized by size or color. The "designer" items are on a rack behind the register. I have gotten a brand-new pair of short Stuart Weitzman boots there for $40 and my friend bought a Louis Vuitton shoulder bag (the strap needed fixing) for $80. I've seen Chanel sneakers for $40, but it's very hit or miss.

Manhattan
1430 Third Avenue between 81st & 82nd Streets
212-772-8810

> Mass transit
> #4, 5, 6, - 86th Street
> For discount parking check out http://www.bestparking.com and http://www.iconparking.com

MEMORIAL SLOAN KETTERING CANCER CENTER THRIFT SHOP of MSKCC

A few doors down from the Arthritis Thrift Shop is Sloan Kettering's. They carry clothing and accessories. Their prices are equivalent to a resale shop, but they do have high quality stock. The designer items are in a back room. They also get donations of manufacturers' samples and have had ten new Vera Wang gowns that were $100 each. They would have been perfect as a bridesmaids' dress.

Manhattan
1440 Third Avenue between 81st & 82nd Streets
212-535-1250

> Mass transit
> #4, 5, 6, - 86th Street

> For driving directions check http://www.mapquest.com
> For discount parking check out http://www.bestparking.com and http://www.iconparking.com

COUNCIL THRIFT SHOP

Run by the National Council of Jewish Women, this shop does not have a large selection of clothing, but, what they have is good quality with designers like Escada and Cole Haan represented. I recently spotted a pair of bronze ankle strap Manolo's at $65.

They are closed on Sunday and don't open until 11:00 a.m.. Monday through Friday.

246 East 84th Street near Second Avenue

212-439-8373

> Mass transit
> #4, 5, 6 - 86th Street
>
> For driving directions check http://www.mapquest.com
> For discount parking check out http://www.bestparking.com
> and http://www.iconprking.com
>
> Restaurant (for the shops on page 89).
> Atlantic Grill
> 1341 Third Avenue at 77th Street
> 212-988-9200
> http://www.brguestrestaurants.com/restaurants/atlantic_grill/index.php
> See description on page 64.

HOUSING WORKS

http://housingworks.org/

Housing Works ' mission is to end the crisis of homelessness and AIDS through the provision of services. They regularly partner with stores like Bloomingdale's offering promotions such as "donate a pair of boots to Housing Works and receive 20% off your new boot purchase at Bloomingdale's".

Check their website for events and promotions.

They have twelve locations throughout the city and stock clothing, furniture, home accessories and books. Their clothing is well priced and their merchandise current and in gently used condition.

LOCATIONS

Manhattan

2569 Broadway between 96th & 97th Streets

212-222-3550

> Mass transit
> #1, 2, 3 - 96th Street
> #1 - 103rd Street
> A, B, C - 96th Street

245 West 10th Street

> Mass transit
> #1, 2 - Christopher St - Sheridan Square
> A, B, C, D, E, F, M - West 4th Street
> #1,2 - Houston Street

143 West 17th Street

718-838-5050

> Mass transit
> #1, 2 - 18th Street
> F, M - 14th Street
> L - 6th Avenue

157 East 23rd Street

212-529-5955

> Mass transit
> #4, 6, 6X - 23rd Street or 28th Street
> N, R - 23rd Street

306 Columbus Avenue at 74th Street.

212-579-7566

> Mass transit
> #1, 2, 3, A, B, C - 72nd Street

730-732 9th Avenue between 49th & 50th Streets

646-963-2665

> Mass transit
> #1, 2, A, C, E - 50th Street
> N, Q, R - 49th Street

130 Crosby Street near Houston Street
646-786-1200
> Mass transit
> B, D, F, M - Broadway - Lafayette Street
> N, R - Prince Street
> #4, 6, 6X - Bleecker Street

119 Chambers Street between W. Broadway & Church
212-732-0584
> Mass transit
> #1, 2, 3, A, C - Chambers Street

202 East 77th Street
212-772-8461
> Mass transit
> #4, 6, 6X - 77th Street or 68th Street - Hunter College
>
> Restaurant
> Atlantic Grill
> 1341 Third Avenue at 77th Street
> 212-988-9200
> See description on page 64.

Brooklyn
266 5th Avenue
718.636.2271
> Mass transit
> D, N, R - Union Street

122 Montague Street
718-237-0521
> Mass transit
> #2, 3, N, R - Court Street
> #2, 3 - Clark Street or Borough Hall

UNIQUE THRIFT
http://unique-thrift-stores.com/index.php

Unique is fairly new to the scene. The Westbury, Long Island location is a huge well lit and laid out space, though the florescent lighting does nothing for the complection. The racks are organized by category and are not packed to the gills, so sorting through them is easy. The merchandise is in very good condition, and some items still have their original tags. They also provide shopping carts for your selections. Signage is in English and Spanish. Dressing rooms are private, large and have full length mirrors.

Their merchandise mix includes men's, women's and children's clothing, accessories, linens, bric-a-brac, furniture toys, and books.

You can sign up for a free Unique VIP card that gives you 25% off on Thursdays. Mondays are always 25% off. They regularly run 50% off sales for VIP members and if you have a Unique card they will email you when those special sales take place.

Regarding their prices - they're very well priced even without the discounts. I've spotted Stuart Weitzman shoes, ABS dresses, Plenty (by Tracey Reese) of which I snagged two silk skirts at $5 each. I've also found a men's Coogi sweater priced at $10. They know their major brands, but not the more esoteric ones, like Free People. Shoes in general run about $6. Like other stores of this ilk, repeated trips increase your chances of scoring a treasure.

They are in the process of opening other locations and do have a number of sites in New Jersey.
Return policy
No exchanges or returns. Cash or credit cards, no checks.

LOCATIONS
Bronx
218 West 234th Street
718-548-1190
Mass transit
#1 - 238th Street

Brooklyn
408 Fulton Street
718-643-1825

Mass transit
F, A - Jay Street - Borough Hall
G - Hoyt - Schermerhorn

Jamaica, Queens
162-10 Jamaica Avenue
347-901-5750
Mass transit
E, J, Z - Jamaica Center-Parsons/Archer

Westbury, Long Island
525 Old Country Road
516-338-1760
Mass transit
LIRR - Westbury
Walk south on Post Avenue to Old Country Road. Unique is
just past the Holy Rood Cemetery (about 2 blocks east).
For driving directions check http://www.mapquest.com

Restaurants
Blimpie - right next door

Café Baci
1636 Old Country Road
See description on page 3.

Levittown, Long Island
3041 Hempstead Turnpike
516-731-1727

THE JUNIOR LEAGUE THRIFT SHOP

This shop has been run by the Junior League for 55 years. Their
mission statement is " . . . an organization of women committed...
voluntarism and improving communities . . . "

They accept donations and carry men's, women's and children's
clothing and accessories. They've been written up in the New York
Times who stated, "In addition to donations from the public and from
members each Junior Leaguer is required to pay membership dues

and donate $250 in merchandise and six hours of time to the shop each year -- major companies, including Tommy Hilfiger and the Worth Collection, often send new surplus clothing." The shop is nicely laid out, and not crowded. Closed Sunday.

<u>Roslyn, Long Island</u>
1395 Old Northern Boulevard
516-621-4800
>For driving directions check http://www.mapquest.com

>Restaurants
>Diane's Trattoria
>21 Bryant Avenue - Roslyn
>516- 621-2591
>See description on page 76.

>Diane's Bakery
>23 Bryant Avenue - Roslyn
>516- 621-2522

>MP Taverna
>http://www.mptaverna.com
>1363 Old Northern Boulevard - Roslyn
>516-686-6486
>See description on page 77.

>Bistro Citron
>1382 Old Northern Boulevard
>516-403-4400
>See description page 77.

<u>Huntington, Long Island</u>
COMMUNITY THRIFT SHOP
http://www.fsl-li.org/programs/familyservices_The_Community_Thrif
tShop.php

The Community Thrift Shop in Huntington is run by the Family Services League. I have found them VERY hit or miss, but many shoppers love them. Most of what they carry is basic clothing, though, I have spied a Pucci skirt that I snagged for $3 (it was 50% off). I've seen shoppers walking through the store with their internet connections up and running checking to see what items were worth on eBay.

Closed Sunday.

274 New York Avenue
631-271-4883

CHAPTER 12

CUT FROM THE SAME CLOTH
Fabric

ACCOUTERMENTS
Trims, Beads, Feathers, Crystals, etc.

"When a person is in fashion, all they do is right."
-Lord Chesterfield

CUT FROM THE SAME CLOTH
Fabric

I've included fabric and trim resources in the guide, as you don't have to know how to sew like Betsy Ross, operate a sewing machine or even thread a needle to create an item from fabric. A pashmina is merely a length of fabric 80" long by either 28" or 36" wide. Buy a fabulous cut of gossamer silk chiffon, rip the finished edges (the selvage) off of each side and rip across the top and bottom for a straight edge and you've got a great shawl! Or find a Chanel look wool boucle and fringe the edges. For a fraction of the cost of a store bought pashmina, you have a fabulous wrap. In fact, many of the fabrics are 60" wide and you can get two pashminas out of an 80" cut.

I've also done wrap skirts (like a sarong) measuring 25" long by 72" around. Rip or fringe the edges, wrap and pin (use a fun brooch) and then pleat and pin. Not one stitch sewn by either machine or hand. And these skirts pack beautifully. (See pages 103 and 104 for photos and instructions.)

As a designer, the garment district, was my stomping ground. Fabric, trim and notions stores line the streets.

Probably the most famous fabric store thanks to "Project Runway" is Mood. But the area, the Garment District, from 35th to 41st Streets between Seventh and Eighth Avenues has a large selection of fabric stores from which to choose.

Ask for swatches and staple them to the store's business card along with the price. This helps when comparing different stores' stock and it makes backtracking much easier. You don't have to try and remember where you unearthed that incredible re-embroidered peau de soie.

I've listed a sampling of my favorite stores and what they specialize in, if applicable. These stores operate like the Grand Bazaar in Istanbul, in that bargaining is the rule of thumb. So hone your skills before you set out and don't dress to impress.

Mass transit

#1 - Times Square - 42nd Street
#2, 3, 7, A, C, E, S, N, Q, R, W - 7th Avenue & 42nd Street
#7, B, D, F, V - 42nd Street - 5th Avenue - 6th Avenue
(PATH) - 33rd Street
For driving directions check http://www.mapquest.com
For discount parking check out http://www.bestparking.com
and http://www.iconparking.com

Manhattan
MOOD FABRICS
http://www.moodfabrics.com

Mood Fabrics was made famous by "Project Runway" as the store that all of their designers buy the fabrics to fashion their creations. They have a wide selection of fabrics, trims, buttons and notions; everything from burnout and lasercut to duchesse satin and organza. The store is well laid out easy to shop. You can also shop online.

Say hello to Swatch, the dog, the store mascot!
Closed Sunday.

225 West 37th Street - 3rd floor
212-730-5003

WEAVERS FABRIC

They have the best selection of Dupionni silk. Marvelous jewel tone colors and interesting woven patterns.
Closed Sunday.

258 West 39th Street between Seventh & Eighth Avenues
212-840-1492

PARON WEST
http://paronfabrics.com/
Their back room stocks a large selection of fabrics at 50% off. They invite you to come in and fondle their fabrics. Open 7 days.

257 West 39th Street corner of Eighth Avenue
212-768-3266

SPANDEX HOUSE
http://www.spandexhouse.com/

If it stretches, they have it! They say they have the largest selection of spandex in the world. Everything from bamboo spandex (for those of you who like to be green), to hologram prints, fishnet and stretch pleather.

Buy a fabulous tropical spandex print and wrap it around your swimsuit. A perfect sarong for the Hampton's, St. Bart's or sunbathing on a Manhattan rooftop.

263 West 38th Street between Seventh & Eighth Avenues
212-354-6711
Closed Sunday.

AYAZMOON FABRIC

They have a large selection of Asian motif brocades, both in rayon and silk. They also sell scarf blocks (36" square silks that can be used as a scarf). I've bought a gorgeous Ferragamo block in cream silk chiffon for $7. Open 7 days.

214B West 39th Street between Seventh & Eighth Avenues
212-869-3315

PRIME FABRICS
http://www.primefabrics.com/

Interesting selection of fabrics at great prices, including designer fabrics..

212 West 35th Street between Seventh & Eighth Avenues
212-465-0780

ACCOUTERMENTS

Trims, beads, feathers, crystals, etc.

DAYTONA TRIMMING
http://www.daytonatrim.com

Check out Daytona for a large selection of trims, buttons, ribbons, flowers, braids and sequins at reasonable prices.

251 West 39th Street between Seventh & Eighth Avenues
212-354-1713

B & Q
http://www.shinetrim.com
http://www.b-qtrimmings.com

B&Q carries sequins, beads, rhinestones, Swarovski crystals, feathers, embroideries, "silk" flowers, ribbon, hat forms. A dizzying collection of sparkle, glitter and glitz.
Closed Sunday.

210 West 38th Street between Seventh & Eighth Avenues
212-398-0988

HAI'S TRIMMING INC.

Like B&Q, Hai's carries sequins, beads, rhinestones, Swarovski crystals, feathers, embroideries, "silk" flowers, ribbons.

242 West 38th Street between Seventh & Eighth Avenues
212-764-2166

Restaurants
Pret a Manger
1410 Broadway at 39th Street
Closed Sunday

See description page 19.
530 Seventh Avenue at 39th Street
Closed Saturday & Sunday.

Café Metro
530 Seventh Avenue between 38th & 39th Streets
(212) 398-8788
See description page 20.

BATHROOM BREAK
The W hotel on Eighth Avenue and 43th Street has a great bathroom.
Walk in like you're a guest, go up the escalator and turn right. If you
look like you belong they won't question you.
270 West 43rd Street, at Eighth Avenue.

IT'S A WRAP

Fabric should be 72" long by whatever length you'd like. Fabric widths typically run 44/45"; 54" or 60" wide. You need 2 yards for the wrap skirt.

Figure 1

Figure 2

Figure 3

Figure 4

Figure 1   Wrap fabric around body.

Figure 2   Pin top fabric to under fabric with decorative brooch.

Figure 3   Wrap remainder of fabric and pleat two or three times. Secure with a decorative brooch.

Figure 4   close up.

CHAPTER 13

ONCE IN A FUCHSIA MOON
Sometimes sales

"Fashion anticipates, and elegance is a state of mind . . . a mirror of the time in which we live, a translation of the future, and should never be static."
-Oleg Cassini

ONCE IN A FUCHSIA MOON
Sometimes sales

A number of charitable organizations hold yearly sales as a way to raise money. I've listed a few of the stand outs.

Check out your local church, synagogue or senior center. Many have occasional sales, especially around the holidays.

THE POSH SALE AT THE LIGHTHOUSE INTERNATIONAL
http://www.lighthouse.org/news-events/events/posh/posh-event-info

One of the social events on the New York scene, the Posh Sale (that raises money for the blind) preview party is regularly featured in the New York Times with photographs of its attendees by New York Times photographer, Bill Cunningham.

Held once a year in May, this four-day sale charges for admittance; $10 per day; $30 for a four-day pass; $175 for the benefit preview party the night prior to opening to the public.

The POSH Sale has been a New York leading fashion fundraiser for almost 40 years. The sale includes fashions for women, men and children from, for example, Asprey, Balenciaga, Burberry, Christian Lacroix, Coach, Courreges, Dior, Dolce & Gabbana, Diane von Furstenberg, Giorgio Armani, Jimmy Choo, Lanvin, Matthew Williamson, Narciso Rodriguez, Oscar de la Renta, Roberto Cavalli, Stella McCartney, Tory Burch and more! Inventory is replenished daily.

The sale can get a bit hectic with multiple women sometimes vying for the same fabulous Valentino gown.

They do not accept checks.

Manhattan
110 East 60th Street between Park & Lexington Avenues

Mass transit
#4, 5, 6, N, R, W - 59th Street & Lexington Avenue
E - Lexington Avenue & 53rd Street
F - 63rd Street & Lexington Avenue

For driving directions check http://www..mapquest.com
For discount parking check out http://www.bestparking.com
and http://www.iconparking.com

LONG ISLAND

GRENVILLE BOYS & GIRLS CLUB SALE
http://www.facebook.com/clothingsalegbbgcl

This little known sale is in its 48th year and runs for a week in May. Shoppers start lining up at 9:00 a.m. for the 10:00 a.m. opening on Friday. Donors receive a pass to shop on Thursday.

The racks are stuffed to bursting and divided into categories. You need strength in your arms to sort through the racks, so pump some iron before you arrive. Sweater, pants and skirts are laid out on long tables and stacked two feet high, with even more items in boxes beneath the tables. The sale is replenished daily with new items.

They have a "boutique" section with jewelry and handbags in glass showcases. Designer clothing is displayed directly behind this. A salesperson must help you with these items. (They help only one person at a time, and have only two or three women staffing this area, so it's slow going)   This is the section that shoppers make a beeline to when the doors open.

The dressing room is communal, so wear something you can strip out of easily and your best undies.

Since many of the sorters and pricers are of the North Shore blue haired crowd, you can sometimes find an esoteric designer that is under priced. They know the major brands and those from the 40s and 50s, but may not be up on Miu Miu or Save the Queen.

As the sale progresses, they start discounting. All blouses $5; handbags for $2, for example. The last day, it's stuff a bag time and they price your purchases by the bagful.

I've gotten a fabulous pair of short, denim and leopard Cavalli boots for $100 (price on the box was more than $400.) The problem is the boots are NOT made for walking, so if I'm going to be sitting most of the evening, they're fine, otherwise, not so much. But then, fashion sometimes pinches.

I also stumbled across a white Chanel pique jacket for $25. It had some stains (that came out in dry cleaning) and was not from a current collection. Since it was a classic style (it had the gold chain sewn on the inside) this was not an issue. I still don't know why they priced it at that bargain price.

At the latest sale I've gotten two pair of Manolo's; a black Mary Jane pair of heels ($18) and a pair of mustard colored flats with eyelets ($28).

HINT: Make sure you bring a large bag to stash your booty in prior to hitting the dressing room.
They take cash and credit cards.

Locust Valley, Long Island
135 Forest Avenue
Locust Valley
516-759-5437 ext. 11

    Mass transit
    LIRR to Locust Valley, Oyster Bay line (about 65 minutes from Penn).
    This line does not have regular trains so check your return time.

    The Club is a three minute walk from the train. Get off the train and walk to the back towards Weirs Lane. Walk up the street and the Club is on your left.

    For driving directions check http://www.mapquest.com

<u>Restaurant</u>
Buckrum Stables
31 Forest Avenue
Locust Valley
516-671-3080
See description page 76.

NOTES

"All women's dresses, in every age and country, are merely variations on the eternal struggle between the admitted desire to dress and the unadmitted desire to undress.
~Lin Yutang

CHAPTER 14

SAMPLE SALES
Have I got a deal for you

"Fashion is a tool ... to compete in life outside the home. People like you better, without knowing why, because people always react well to a person they like the looks of."
-Mary Quant - designer

SAMPLE SALES
Have I got a deal for you

I'm not a fan of sample sales. That said, as you walk through the garment district, especially at the end of the season (which is a season ahead of what is in the stores), you'll see people on street corners handing out flyers for sample sales. The items in the sale represent leftover showroom samples and/or overstock. It's a great way for a company to make some extra cash and sometimes for you to get a deal. Be aware that in most cases, you can't try on, there are no returns and some sales are cash only.

Two experiences that I had turned me off to sample sales. I went with a friend to a sample sale of a company whose things I loved. The sale was at their warehouse in the bowels of New Jersey. After spending more than two hours driving in rush hour traffic, I ended up with only a green leather belt (which is probably still in my closet somewhere).

My other experience was buying a skirt and a strapless midriff top from a hat company that had taken the plunge into ready to wear. Big mistake. The skirt was a mid-calf, multi-patterned chintz, gored and godeted, really cute. No try-ons. The problem was the skirt was really tapered at the knee which restricted walking to the extent that it caused you to walk like a penguin. This is fine if you're making a guest appearance in "Happy Feet"; not so fine if you actually need to walk. The motto of this experience is that hat companies may know heads, but not so much bodies.

TOP BUTTON
This website will email you sample sales scheduled for the coming week.
http://www.topbutton.com/Home/

SOIFFER HASKIN
Check out their site for pop up samples sales throughout New York City.
http://www.soifferhaskin.com/Home.aspx

CHAPTER 15

CANAL STREET & CHINATOWN
Fee-Fi-Faux-Fum, I spy a bag
by Louis Vuitton

"Fashion is not something that exists in dresses only. Fashion is in the sky, in the street, fashion has to do with ideas, the way we live, what is happening."
-Coco Chanel

CANAL STREET & CHINATOWN
Fee- Fi-Faux-Fum, I spy a bag by Louis Vuitton

The area between Chinatown and Little Italy is like Madison Avenue for those of us with a limited budget. Known far and wide (just have a listen to all of the languages spoken around you) as the knock-off center of New York, Canal Street sports copies of many of the elite brands sold on Madison Avenue. Shopping on Canal is akin to perusing the souk in Marrakech; it's chaotic and crowded.

Situated in lower Manhattan, on Canal Street and Broadway are small stalls that carry everything from bags, watches, perfume and tee shirts, to sunglasses, scarves, shawls and shoes. Welcome to Canal Street, the bazaar for the price conscious fashionista to shop for cheap and affordable faux brand name designer bags and other merchandise. While an original "Louis" bag could be upwards of $1,500, the knock-off might be $30. Obviously, the quality is not the same, but it's your choice and your pocketbook (excuse the pun).

As many of the vendors are selling knock-offs, I am not listing them here as they tend to be a bit skittish about being busted. It's illegal to sell knock-offs. But for the consumer, Roger E. Schechter, professor of law at George Washington University stated, "It's illegal to sell, but not to buy." So if you do purchase that Prada handbag, you won't end up in the pokie.

Canal is best for handbags, watches and sunglasses. Do not buy perfume there, it's not the same as the original.

There will be sellers lining the street who will whisper to you, their mantra: "Handbag Chanel, Coach, Louis Vuitton, Prada inside." A few may have a brochure of what they carry. They will lead you to a secret location to show you their wares. Through the woods to grandmother's house we go, so to speak. But instead of a cup of grandma's cocoa, you'll find a showroom of faux designer merchandise. Through dark alleys, into office buildings, up elevators, down corridors. Be aware that when they tell you that their showroom is right around the corner, it could be a twenty minute walk.

Some of the stall holders on Canal (the stalls are signless, three-sided and long, but very narrow, (only about five feet wide) will have their faux merchandise hidden somewhere in their stall and if you don't look like a federale, they'll whip it out. Some companies, like Louis Vuitton and Chanel, are more aggressive about enforcement, others a bit more lax. So you may see Coach bags front and center, but LV and Chanel will usually be stashed away.

Quality varies dramatically and the price follows suit. Bargaining is the name of the game. The price goes down as you start walking away. I had one vendor quote me $40 for sunglasses. As I was leaving, he came down to $8! But, usually the spread is not that vast. You have to decide what that Prada bag is worth to you and aim for that number.

The vendors have an early warning system, via cell phone and if a bust is imminent, they will bring down their stall gates. Years ago, my sister and her two young children got stuck inside a stall when the "alarm" went out and the gates were pulled shut. The kids are grown now, but still talk about the experience.

Crackdowns on the vendors occur sporadically and make them a bit gun shy. So instead of actually having the merchandise on hand they will show a potential customer a photo of the requested item or pull up a picture on a website. If you like the photo they will send a runner to bring you the handbag (usually meeting you on a street corner.)

A nice perk on Canal Street are the many mani/pedi/massage options. For a fraction of what it would cost at the Canyon Ranch Spa you can rejuvenate with a quick massage. Cost: $40 for 60 minutes.

TIP
Don't dress to the nines when shopping Canal. Leave your furs and "diamonds" at home. The vendors size you up when quoting a price.

Hold onto your wallet; the streets are crowded and the stalls are very narrow which makes for optimum conditions for pick pocket activity, though I've never had a problem.

Mass transit
#4, 5, 6, N, R - Canal Street

For driving directions check http://www.mapquest.com
For discount parking check out http://www.bestparking.com
and http://www.iconparking.com

Restaurants
Il Cortile Ristorante Italiano
http://www.ilcortile.com
125 Mulberry Street
212-226-6060

Calm in the midst of a storm . . .   A lovely respite from the
chaos of Canal. A sky lit dining room that feels like you're
dining al fresco in Italy. Be sure and ask for the Power Lunch
menu (available Monday through Saturday), as items are a
fraction of the cost of those listed on their regular menu. The
food is wonderful and you'll leave fortified to battle the hoards
again.

Positano
http://www.positanooflittleitaly.com
122 Mulberry Street between Canal and Hester Streets
212-334-9808

After shopping Canal and Soho treat yourself to a plate of
fabulous carb boosting pasta. Their Shrimp Francese is to
die for. And don't forget to leave room for an Italian pastry.

M & B Fu Kee
128 Lafayette Street
212- 965-9410

Walk down to Lafayette Street. This Chinese restaurant
caters mostly to locals. The food is tasty and plentiful with
dishes like chicken and vegetables costing about $6. The
bathroom leaves a bit to be desired though. Bring your own
toilet paper. Fu Kee is good for a fast refuel before hitting the
streets again.   Sbarro

298 Canal Street
See description page 26.

For a quick bit of sustenance, try this pizza chain. They serve slices, salads and pastas. An extra bonus is a nice bathroom; though there's usually a line.

Il Palazzo
151 Mulberry Street
212-343-7000
A little bit of Italy... Their fried calamari is among the best I've had, light and tender

Mulberry Project
http://www.mulberryproject.com
149 Mulberry Street
646-448-4536

Right next door to Il Palazzo. Walk down a flight of stairs to what looks like a cellar and discover Mulberry Project. A bar/club that serves light snacks and interesting concoctions of drinks. Very young and hip. It has a lovely open air back patio. If your shopping lasts into the evening it's the perfect place for a drink.

BATHROOM BREAK
McDonald's on Canal makes for a good pit stop. They sometimes make you purchase something, though.

Also, try Starbucks on Broadway off Canal Street.

NOTES

"Adornment is never anything except a reflection of the heart."
~ Chanel

CHAPTER 16

OUTLET STORES

"As to matters of dress, I would recommend one never to be first in the fashion nor the last out of it."
John Wesley - English Evangelist, founder of Methodism. 1703-1791

OUTLET STORES

As a rule, I do not shop outlet malls. I don't find that there are any "deals." In the vast majority of cases, the merchandise in the stores is made specifically for the outlet. For instance, they may take a Ralph Lauren polo and dumb it down to hit a certain price point. Some stores stock last season's items, seconds, or leftovers, but that is not the bulk of their stock.

There are two outlets that I do shop - Off Fifth (the Saks Fifth Avenue outlet) and Neiman Marcus' Last Call. Both do have items made for the outlet, but have a large stock of designer clothing and accessories formerly sold at their full price stores.

A word about those Tanger Outlet percentage off coupons that are mailed, online or included with your newspapers. I tried using them recently and was told that if there is already a percentage off sale the coupons cannot be used. My advice if you get these coupons, is to contact the store that you are planning on using it in before going out to the outlet and ask if it actually can be used.

LAST CALL - NEIMAN MARCUS
http://www.neimanmarcus.com/store/info/lastcall.jhtml?storeId=210/DR&icid=LCCDeerPark

I know it's a shlep, but it could be worth your while. Located in The Arches Outlet Mall in Deer Park, Last Call (the Neiman Marcus outlet) carries men's, women's and children's, accessories, jewelry, furniture and decorative home accessories. I've never been there when it was crowded. I park right outside the store, shop and then head out. As I've said, I am not an afficionado of outlet malls

Last Call is upscale and the surrounding area and other stores in the Mall are not of the ilk that usually appeal to an upscale customer. This makes for a good selection for those in the know. Many racks contain merchandise from last season that was sold at Neiman's. Some items are made for the outlet.

They have racks of discounted designer items and a fabulous shoe department. I find that the prices are still a bit on the high side, but you can evaluate for yourself. Evening gowns are final sale.

Deer Park, Long Island
Tanger Outlet Center at The Arches at Deer Park
152 The Arches Circle
631-242-6454

Return policy
30 days with receipt and tags attached - full refund.

> Mass transit
> LIRR - Deer Park
> There are shuttle buses provided from the LIRR station.
> For driving directions check http://www.mapquest.com

SAKS FIFTH AVENUE - OFF FIFTH

The outlet for Saks Fifth Avenue, like Neiman's, has many racks that contain merchandise from last season that were sold at Saks. Some items are made for the outlet. They have racks of discounted designer items, a good shoe department, men's, women's and children's clothing, accessories, jewelry, and decorative home accessories.

One of the Saks outlets is In the same Mall as Last Call.
Return policy
30 days with receipt and tags attached - full refund.

LOCATIONS
Westbury, Long Island
The Gallery at Westbury Plaza
Old Country Road
516-228-2165

> Restaurant
> Café Baci
> Old Country Road - Westbury
> See description page 3.

Deer Park, Long Island
Tanger Outlet Center at The Arches at Deer Park
455 Commack Rd., Suite 1250
631-254-0684

For driving directions check http://www.mapquest.com

WOODBURY COMMON PREMIUM OUTLETS
http://www.premiumoutlets.com/outlets/outlet.asp?id=7

Home to 220 outlet stores including: Burberry, Coach, Chloe, Dunhill, Giorgio Armani, Gucci, J.Crew, Jimmy Choo, Lacoste, Last Call by Neiman Marcus, Nike, Polo Ralph Lauren, Prada, Saks Fifth Avenue Off 5th, Tod's, Tory Burch.

Check their website for travel information.

Central Valley, NY
498 Red Apple Court
(845) 928-4000

SWIMWEAR ANYWHERE
www.swimwearanywhere.com

For driving directions check http://www.mapquest.com

They are the second largest branded swimwear manufacturer in North America and they hold the license to manufacture for Carmen Marc Valvo Swim, DKNY Swim, Juicy Couture Beach, Juicy Couture Beach Baby and Liz Claiborne. They also design Beach House, Coco Reef, Gabar, Matari Mix'ems and Roxanne.

This is more of a company store than an outlet. The small store attached to their manufacturing facility discounts swimsuits and cover-ups by at least 50%. Suit tags are color coded and prices are posted.
Return Policy
All sales final.

Hours:
Tuesday - Friday - 10:00 a.m. to 6:00 p.m.
Saturday - 10:00 a.m. to 4:00 p.m.
They close from 2:00 to 3:00 for lunch.

Farmingdale, Long Island
85 Sherwood Avenue
631-420-1400 ext. - 139

Riverhead, Long Island
TANGER OUTLETS RIVERHEAD
http://www.tangeroutlet.com/riverhead/

Tanger is located in Suffolk Count on Long Island. It carries brands like Bebe, Armani, Barney's, BCBG, Banana Factory Outlet, DKNY, Juicy, Michael Kors, Saks - Off Fifth, Theory and Victoria's Secret, to name a few.

Check their website for the full list, current sales and discounts and directions.

Riverhead
200 Tanger Mall Drive
631-369-2732 or 800-407-4894

NOTES

"Cinderella is proof that a new pair of shoes can change your life.
-Unknown

CHAPTER 17

FASHION JETSETTERS

"I don't design clothes. I design dreams."
-Ralph Lauren

FASHION JETSETTERS
Fly me to the stores

BIJOUX TERNER
http://www.bijouxterner.com/web/guest/home

JFK International Airport - Terminal 4
La Guardia Airport - Terminal B

They were founded in 1974 in Miami and are an international company with a single-price retail concept. They design, source and sell accessories inspired by global fashion trends for women, men and the home with all items in the store tagged at $10. Their research has found that their core target customer is a fashionista.

For those of you who are jetsetters you may have come across Bijoux Terner at the airport, one of the only brick and mortar locations they have. This makes flight delays a bit more bearable. (I've gotten so caught up in shopping that I've almost missed my flight once or twice.) At the airports where everything is so overpriced, Bijoux Terner is a welcome find.

They are also carried by the shops on a number of cruise ships and I've spotted Bijoux Terner in port in the Caribbean.

The quality of their jewelry has gone downhill and some of it is downright tacky, but it's worth a look.

Their handbags and evening bags are offered in a multitude of colors and styles. For ten bucks those with a discriminating eye can unearth a great accessory. How can you go wrong for that price?

CHAPTER 18

ESTATE & GARAGE SALES
They couldn't take it with them but you can

TAG SALES & GARAGE SALES
Yours, mine, ours

"A woman's dress should be like a barbed- wire fence: serving its purpose without obstructing the view."
-Sophia Loren

ESTATE SALES
They couldn't take it with them, but you can

GARAGE & TAG SALES
Yours, mine, ours

Shopping at estate, tag and garage sales is like a treasure hunt. You never know what you'll dig out of a filled to bursting basement.

Estate/Tag Sales
The most common reason for an Estate Sale is the death of the property owner. These sales usually encompass the contents of the entire house and are run by professionals, who sometimes know and sometimes do not know what things are worth. Most professionals are well versed in furniture, artwork, bric-a-brac and carpets and often not knowledgeable about clothing and accessories. I've snagged some treasures at professionally run estate and tag sales and I didn't have to get up at the crack of dawn.

I've found a Hermes scarf for $8, thrown into a wicker basket with a bunch of other scarves; a great vintage silk blouse patterned with the streets of Paris for $5. I also love vintage handbags from the 1950s and they are usually priced between $5 and $10.

Garage & Tag Sales
People run garage or yard sales to get rid of the things they no longer want. But, one woman's trash is another woman's treasure.

A few years ago I came across a garage sale that was like the mother lode. The woman owned a company on Seventh Avenue that made women's and men's clothing, manufacturing private label garments for Saks and Bloomingdale's. Her husband had gone to Asia to oversee the manufacturing, met a local woman and never came back. So the wife closed the business and sold off all of the stock at a garage sale. Everything was $5. (I called her my $5 sweater lady.) She had silk shirts, sweaters, coats, jackets and pants. She ran the sale every weekend for weeks until the neighbors called the police complaining that she was running a business. But in the interim I stocked up on some fabulous items.

I've recently been to a tag sale in a large house in a swanky area. This was another clothing business liquidation. Great funky, trendy clothes that were basically sold by the bagful.

At a garage sale at a modest little house, I purchased a pair of 3" high gold ankle strap Manolo's for $25.

My point in relating these experiences is, you never know what you'll discover, so get out there and hunt.

A good source for estate/tag/garage sale listings is Craigslist. They're also listed in Pennysaver and on Long Island in Newsday.

http://www.craigslist.org/about/sites

http://www.yardsaletreasuremap.com/

http://www.newsday.com/classifieds

NOTES

"If I don't stop shopping, I'll end up a bag lady; a Fendi bag lady, but a bag lady...."
-- Carrie from Sex and the City

CHAPTER 19

ANYWHERE YOU HANG YOUR HAT IS HOME
Hotels in the Big Apple

"One should either be a work of art, or wear a work of art."
~Oscar Wilde

ANYWHERE YOU HANG YOUR HAT IS HOME
Hotels in the Big Apple

For those of you who are visiting the Big Apple, finding a reasonable hotel is one of the first steps in planning your trip.

There are 100,000 rooms in New York City. They run the gamut of those that charge under $100 to those that have a price tag of upwards of $1000.

My recommendation for selecting a hotel is to pick an area in which you feel you will be spending a lot of time (ie-shopping time). I usually stay in midtown between West 34th Street and 59th Street and 5th Avenue to 8th Avenue, as I like to see a play or two in addition to shopping. Find a hotel that is near public transportation (subway and buses). New York has a great mass transit system. They offer daily and weekly passes that are a great deal. Check out the website: http://www.mta.info/mta/fares/mc_value.htm Taxis in Manhattan are slow due to traffic and are pricey. And wouldn't you rather put that extra cash towards a cute pair of shoes?

During peak times (Thanksgiving, Christmas//New Year's, Easter/, Fourth of July), hotel rooms are at a premium and therefore cost more. Off times January, February and March you can find better prices. New York hotels usually offer lower rates on the weekends as the business travelers vacate.

Sign up for Jetsetter's free membership (http://www.jetsetter.com) to be alerted to the best prices. They run sales at a number of hotels and their prices are often less than the hotel charges on their website. I saw a sale for the Essex House on Central Park South and 7th Avenue (great location) at a rate of $235 for September The price listed on the Essex House site as their "Best Available Rate" was $529. Essex House is a very upscale hotel. I've stayed there and it's lovely.

I've also stayed at the Sheraton Manhattan (on Seventh Avenue and 51st Street)) and the New York Hilton (Avenue of the Americas between 53rd and 54th Streets) Wonderful hotels and great locations.

Starwood Hotels - http://www.starwoodhotels.com/sheraton/index.html

Affinia hotels has a number of properties in Manhattan. Some are larger than New York City apartments, boasting a queen bed, pull out queen sleeper sofa in a living room area, a dining table and a fully equipped kitchen (they even have flatware and plates). They also offer a free wine hour at most of their properties which is a nice perk. www.affinia.com I've found that if you keep checking back on the site closer to your reservation date you may find a lower price.

If you're planning on spending more time in the Soho/Lower Broadway area check out hotels there. The Wall Street area hotels often are lower priced than those in midtown.

Another resource for uncovering a discount price on a hotel is www.groupon.com and www.travelzoo.com Both regularly post offers for New York City hotels that are lower than the hotel's best rate. Purchase a voucher from the site and you usually have six months to use it. They also offer restaurant vouchers.

After I select a hotel I always check Tripadvisor for the hotels' ratings. I have never been disappointed. http://www.tripadvisor.com

For mass transit directions from one subway stop to another click on https://www.hopstop.com/ For the latest events go to http://www.nycgo.com/

A word about New York hotel rooms and size. Most of the rooms (unless you upgrade to a suite) are SMALL. But since you're out and about most of the day and night (New York is the "city that never sleeps") I don't really use size as a criteria.

Feel like a three course meal at a cut rate price? Check out http://www.restaurant.com You can purchase a $10 to $100 voucher for between $2 and $40. Make sure you read the small print regarding when you can use it.

Check out http://www.savored.com for percentage off (15%-40%) at New York restaurants. Some top restaurants participate.

<u>NOTES</u>

"I don't shop because I need something, I just shop for shopping's sake."
-- Cat Deeley

CHAPTER 20

WEBSITES/RESOURCES
Online Shopping
Bookstores
Designer sites
Trend sites

"One had as good be out of the world, as out of the fashion."

-Colley Cibber - English Actor and Playwright, 1671-1757

WEBSITES
Be in the fashion know
Online Shopping
Designers
Trend Sites

I've compiled a list of websites dedicated to online shopping, specific designers and the latest fashion trends.

I am not an online shopper. I like to see the garment up close and personal, feel the fabric and try the item on. For me, it's part of the shopping experience. But, for those of you who do shop online, the sites listed offer great deals and many designers in the better priced market are cutting special runs for some of these sites.

A well-informed fashionista makes a better shopper, so I've listed sites for both trends and designers. Every dedicated follower of fashion should be plugged into the top designers and the latest trends,

You can catch up on the latest trends at:

AROUND THE WORLD FASHION PUBLICATIONS
http://www.shop.aroundtheworldnyc.com

This store located in the garment district carries a huge assortment of fashion magazines from around the world. It is where designers go to buy publications picturing the latest trends. A fabulous resource.

148 West 37th Street
212-695-2534

ONLINE SHOPPING

BLUEFLY
http://www.bluefly.com

One of the original online discount designer sites that came on the scene during the .com boom of the '90s and is still going strong. They have an extensive selection of designer merchandise at up to 80% off retail.

ARDEN B
http://www.ardenb.com/home.jsp

They used to have a few brick and mortar stores in the New York area, but they are no longer operating, so I've added their online information.

I love their styling. It's sexy and feminine, suitable for the office or a hot night out on the town.

They reinterpret the latest high fashion styles at prices that are easy on the budget.

Their great prices become even better when they run a sale, which they regularly do. "Buy one get one free"; "Buy one get one for $15"; "50%-65% off"; "$5 clearance," etc.

They also have a B.rewarded membership program.
Return policy
30 days

IDEELI
http://www.ideeli.com/
You sign up for free membership and they post sales each day that start at 12 p.m. EST. The sales last 40 hours, or until items are sold out. They offer up to 80% off designer and bridge lines. They will send you daily emails of the latest offerings.

HAUTE LOOK
http://www.hautelook.com/events
Another sign up for free membership site with trendy items at up to 75% off retail. They will send you daily emails describing their sales.

RUE LA LA

http://www.ruelala.com/

Sign up for membership (free) and shop for brands like Sue Wong, Betsey Johnson and Judith Ripka. They carry premium branded items at boutiques that are open for just a brief window of time.

GILT GROUPE

http://www.gilt.com/

Gilt Groupe grants you exclusive access to sales of designer gear and accessories, at up to 70% off. You have to request membership and they will send you an email when you are accepted.

DESIGNERS

www.agnesb.com
www.mulberry.com
www.giorgioarmani.com
www.donnakaran.com
www.viviennetam.com
www.Gucci.com
www.prada.com
www.chanel.com
www.alexandermcqueen.com
www.aquascutum.co.uk
www.viviennetam.com
www.viviennewestwood.com
www.valentino.com
www.dior.com
www.paulandjoe.com
www.bluemarine.com
www.albertaferretti.com

www.joyce.com
www.ralphlauren.com
www.emporioarmani.com
www.louisvuitton.com
www.burberry.com
www.savethequeen.com
www.annasui.com
www.miumiu.com
www.versace.com
www.marcjacobs.com
www.loewe.com
www.celine.com
www.moschino.com
www.katharinehamnett.com
www.givenchy.com
www.lanvin.com
www.soniarykiel.com

TREND SITES

www.fashionmission.nl/Fashion-Designers--0001980002.dfs
An A to Z listing for designer collections and trend info.

http://www.fashionfromspain.com
Features the latest fashion designs from Spain, a calender of events, pictures from fashion shows, and links to other similar sites.

http://www.fashioncapital.co.uk/
Provides in-depth descriptions of future fashion trends. They have different sections for women's and menswear and descriptions of trends focusing on fabric, color, cut and detail. In the section of the site referred to as "Fashion Gallery" one can browse fashion from all different parts of the globe, look at textiles, find listings of fashion periodicals and books and reviews of fashion exhibitions in London.

http://www.123world.com/fashions
A source for information about the fashion houses of the world on the net. It will directly take you to the official homepage of the particular fashion house.

http://www.fashionalley.net/
Articles on trends and styles.

http://www.fashionweekdaily.comOffers the latest runway reports along with live runway shows
featuring the latest trends from fashion week. It's the fashion insider's bible.

http://www.FGI.org
The Fashion Group International is a global nonprofit association representing all areas of the fashion, apparel, accessories, beauty and home industries.

http://www.firstview.com/
It highlights designer collections from A to Z. There is a subscription fee.

http://www.fashion.net/fashion/
A link for designers, labels, magazines, books, blogs, mailers, job listings.

NOTES

"Fashion is very important. It is life enhancing and, like everything that gives pleasure, it is worth doing well."
-Vivienne Westwood

CHAPTER 21

FOLLOW THE YELLOW BRICK ROAD
Planning your shopping route
Stores and restaurants by area

"The only rule is don't be boring and dress cute wherever you go. Life is too short to blend in."
-Paris Hilton

AREA MAP OF MANHATTAN

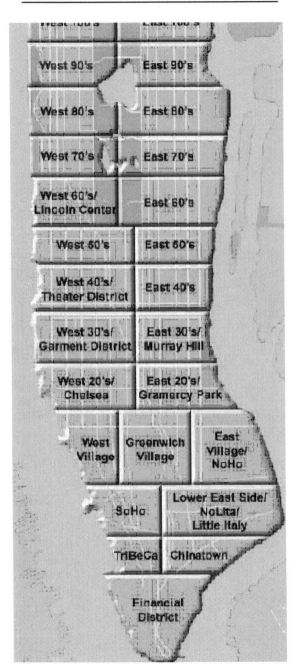

FOLLOW THE YELLOW BRICK ROAD
Planning your shopping route
Stores and restaurants by area

I've grouped clusters of stores in a particular area to make your shopping forays more efficient. You may have to do a bit of backtracking to hit all the stores. Most are listed from the lowest address to the highest. Restaurants are also grouped by area.

WALL STREET AREA

CENTURY 21
22 Cortlandt Street between Broadway & Church Street

DSW SHOES
Battery Park
102 North End Avenue

KNOW STYLE
80 Nassau Street at Fulton Street

HOUSING WORKS
119 Chambers Street

T.J. MAXX
14 Wall Street

STRAWBERRY
253B Warren Street

LOWER MANHATTAN
CANAL STREET, LOWER BROADWAY, SOHO, RIVINGTON

FOREVER 21
568 Broadway between Houston & Prince Streets

MARMALADE VINTAGE
174 Mott Street at Broome Street

EDITH MACHINIST
104 Rivington Street off Ludlow Street

NARNIA
161 Rivington Street between Clinton and Suffolk

SECOND TIME AROUND
111 Thompson Street
262 Mott Street

STELLA DALLAS
218 Thompson Street

HOUSING WORKS
130 Crosby Street at Houston Street

H & M
558 Broadway
515 Broadway between Spring and Broome Streets

MYSTIQUE
547 Broadway between Spring & Prince Streets
368 Broadway between Walker & Canal Streets

NECESSARY CLOTHING
442-443 Broadway between Howard and Grand Streets
676 Bleeker Street

TOPSHOP
478 Broadway at Broome Street

AMSTERDAM BOUTIQUE
454 Broadway Between Howard & Grand Streets

STRAWBERRY
253 Warren Street

Continue walking down Broadway to Canal Street. You can then hit the vendors on Canal.

Restaurants for Lower Manhattan

Lure
142 Mercer Street off Prince Street

40 Carrots @ Bloomingdale's
504 Broadway between Broome and Spring Streets

Il Cortile
125 Mulberry Street
Positano
122 Mulbery Street

Il Palazzo
151 Mulberry Street

Mulberry Project
149 Mulberry Street

Sbarro
415 Broadway

Sbarro
298 Canal Street

M & B Fu Kee
128 Lafayette Street

CHELSEA, FLATIRON, EAST VILLAGE
Below 34th Street -Third to Seventh Avenue

MYSTIQUE
324 Fifth Avenue between 32nd & 33rd Streets

HOUSING WORKS
157 East 23rd Street

STRAWBERRY
286 First Avenue at 17th Street

BRIDAL GARDEN
54 West 21st Street - Ste. 907 near Avenue of the Americas

KLEINFELD
110 West 20th Street

H & M
111 Fifth Avenue at 18th Street

HOUSING WORKS
143 West 17th Street

MARSHALLS
620 Avenue of the Americas between 18th & 19th Streets

SECOND TIME AROUND
94 Seventh Avenue between 15th and 16th Streets

DSW SHOES
Union Square
40 East 14th Street off Fifth Avenue

T.J. MAXX
40 East 14th Street
620 Avenue of The Americas at 18th Street

FOREVER 21
40 East 14th Street between Broadway & University Place

STRAWBERRY
38 East 14th Street

BEACON'S CLOSET
10 West 13th Street

BUFFALO EXCHANGE
East Village
332 East 11th Street between First & Second Avenues

Restaurants for Chelsea, Flatiron, East Village

Tocqueville.
1 East 15th Street

Le Pain Quotidien
38 East 19th Street between Broadway & Park Avenues

WEST SIDE

Broadway - 28th to 33rd Street

NORLHA
1179 Broadway between 27th & 28th Streets

JEWELRY HOUSE CORP.
42 West 28th Street between 6th Avenue & Broadway

PERLA DESIGNS
57 West 28th Street

FOREVER FASHION OF NYC
109 West 28th Street off Broadway

P & K JEWELRY
1201 Broadway (between 28th & 29th Streets)

JEWELRY IN TREND
1204 Broadway between 29th & 30th Streets
59 West 31st Street

DRANGO SPHERE INC.
151A West 30th Street

PERFUME
 Broadway between 30th & 31st Streets

NIMA
1235 Broadway 2nd floor

U. S. JEWELRY HOUSE LTD.
42 West 28th Street between 6th Avenue and Broadway

EARRINGS PLAZA
1263 Broadway between 30th & 31st Streets

STRAWBERRY
901 6th Avenue at 32nd Street

Restaurants for West Side
Ayza
11 West 31st Street off Broadway

Fresh Food
Seventh Avenue at West 30th Street

Pret a Manger
342 Seventh Avenue at 29th Street

MIDTOWN WEST
GARMENT DISTRICT
34th Street To 41st Street - Fifth To Ninth Avenue

FOREVER 21
50 West 34th Street & Broadway

STRAWBERRY
14 West 34th Street off Fifth Avenue

PRIMA DONNA
433 Fifth Avenue between 38th & 39th Streets

H & M 1328
Broadway at 34th Street

DSW SHOES
213 West 34th Street

CONWAY
245 West 34th Street between Seventh & Eighth Avenues

CONWAY
450 Seventh Avenue between 34th and 35th Streets

H & M
435 Seventh Avenue at 34th Street

DZHAVAEL COUTURE
247 West 37th Street between Seventh & Eighth Avenues

CHANTELLE FASHION LTD.
46 West 37th Street between Fifth Avenue & Avenue of the Americas

ELI & COMPANY
207 West 37th Street between Seventh & Eighth Avenues

LILA MADISON
556 Eighth Avenue

ALEXIS D
246 West 37th Street

DESIGN BY NOVA
1000 Avenue of the Americas between 37th & 38th Streets

MOOD FABRICS
235 West 37th Street (3rd fl) between Seventh & Eighth Avenues

MANNY'S MILLINERY SUPPLY
26 West 38th Street between Fifth Avenue & Avenue of the Americas

HAT CESSORY
60 West 38th Street between Fifth Avenue & Avenue of the Americas

B & Q
210 West 38th Street

HAI'S TRIMMING INC.

242 West 38th Street between Seventh & Eighth Avenues

SPANDEX HOUSE
263 West 38th Street between Seventh & Eighth Avenues

WEAVERS FABRIC
258 West 39th Street between Seventh & Eighth Avenues

AYAZMOON FABRIC
214B West 39th Street between Seventh & Eighth Avenues

SHINETRIM
228 West 39th Street - 2nd floor

PARON WEST / PARON ANNEX
257 West 40th Street corner of Eighth Avenue

DAYTONA TRIMMING
251 West 39th Street between Seventh & Eighth Avenues

RK BRIDAL
318 West 39th Street between Eighth & Ninth Avenues

Restaurants for Midtown West, Garment District

Sbarro
159 West 33rd Street at Seventh Avenue

Café Metro
530 Seventh Avenue between 38th & 39th Streets

Pret a Manger
1020 Avenue of the Americas at 38th Street

Pret a Manger
485 Seventh Avenue

Pret a Manger
1410 Broadway at 39th Street

Bryant Park Grill
25 West 40th Street off Avenue of the Americas

MIDTOWN WEST
42nd To 59th Street Fifth Avenue To Ninth Avenue

H & M
4 Times Square
1472 Broadway

FOREVER 21
1540 Broadway at 45th Street

HOUSING WORKS
730-732 9th Avenue

TJ MAXX
250 West 57th Street at Eighth Avenue

STRAWBERRY
1700 Broadway between 53rd and 54th Streets
49 West 57th Street between Fifth and Sixth Avenues

Restaurant for Midtown West - 42nd to 59th Street
Red Eye Grill
890 Seventh Avenue at 56th Street

WEST SIDE
Above 59th Street

CENTURY 21
1972 Broadway between 66th and 67th Streets

SECOND TIME AROUND
238 West 72nd Street
2624 Broadway at 99th Street

FOX'S
2234 Broadway at 80th Street

HOUSING WORKS
306 Columbus Avenue at 74th Street
DSW SHOES
220 Broadway at 79th Street

HOUSING WORKS
2569 Broadway & 96th Street

T.J. MAXX
808 Columbus Avenue near 100th Street

MARSHALLS
Harlem Center
125 West 125th Street between Seventh & Lenox Avenues

Restaurant for West Side above 59th Street
Cosi
2186 Broadway between 76th & 77th Streets

MIDTOWN EAST
42nd To 57th Street - Fifth To Third Avenue

H & M
505 Fifth Avenue at 42nd Street

STRAWBERRY
129 East 42nd Street at Lexington Avenue

H & M
640 5th Ave & 51st Street

Restaurants for Midtown East - 42nd to 59th Street
Sbarro
451 Lexington Avenue between 44th & 45th Streets

Pret a Manger
425 Madison Avenue - 48th Street

Pret a Manger
400 Park Avenue at 54th Street
        Cosi
        60 East 56th Street between Madison & Park Avenues

UPPER EAST SIDE
Above 57th Street

H & M
731 Lexington Avenue and 59th Street

TJ MAXX
407 East 59th Street

SECOND TIME AROUND
1040 Lexington Avenue between 74th and 75th Streets

SYLVIA PINES UNIQUITIES
1102 Lexington Avenue at 77th Street

HOUSING WORKS
202 East 77th Street

MICHAEL'S - CONSIGNMENT SHOP FOR WOMEN
1041 Madison Avenue between 79th & 80th - upstairs

MEMORIAL SLOAN KETTERING CANCER CENTER THRIFT SHOP
of MSKCC
1440 Third Avenue between 81st & 82nd Streets

THE ARTHRITIS THRIFT SHOP
1430 Third Avenue between 81st & 82nd Streets

LA BOUTIQUE RESALE
141 East 62nd Street corner of Lexington Avenue
144 East 74th Street between Second & Third Avenues
1045 Madison Avenue near 80th Street

DESIGNER RESALE & GENTLEMEN'S RESALE

324 East 81st Street between Second & Third Avenues

ENCORE CONSIGNMENT
1132 Madison Avenue between 84th & 85th Streets
2nd & 3rd floors

BIS DESIGNER
1134 Madison Avenue between 84th & 85th Streets

COUNCIL THRIFT SHOP
246 East 84th Street near Second Avenue

H & M
150 East 86th Street & Lexington Avenue.

STRAWBERRY
161 East 86th Street

Restaurants for Upper East Side above 57th Street
40 Carrots @ Bloomingdale's
Lexington Avenue at East 57th Street

Serendipity 3
225 East 60th Street off Third Avenue

Vivolo
140 East 74th Street between Lexington and Park Avenues

Atlantic Grill
1341 Third Avenue at 77th Street

Le Pain Quotidien
1131 Madison Avenue between 84th & 85th Streets

LONG ISLAND

MANHASSET, ROSLYN

MARSHALLS

Manhasset
1380 Northern Boulevard

MYSTIQUE
Manhasset
1583 Northen Boulevard

THE JUNIOR LEAGUE THRIFT SHOP
Roslyn
1395 Old Northern Boulevard

REVIVAL
Roslyn
1374 Old Northern Boulevard

Restaurants for Manhasset, Roslyn
Cipollini
Manhasset
The Americana
2110C Northern Boulevard off Searingtown Road

Diane's Trattoria/Diane's Bakery
Roslyn
21/23 Bryant Avenue

MP Taverna
Roslyn
1363 Old Northern Boulevard

Bistro Citron
Roslyn
1362 Old Northern Boulevard

GARDEN CITY, ROOSEVELT FIELD MALL, CARLE PLACE, WESTBURY
I've grouped these west to east

H & M
Garden City

Roosevelt Field Mall

FOREVER 21
Roosevelt Field
630 Old Country Road - #1124A

DSW SHOES
Carle Place
357 Old Country Road

OFF FIFTH
Westbury
The Gallery at Westbury Plaza

MARSHALLS
Westbury
1240 Old Country Road

UNIQUE THRIFT
Westbury
525 Old Country Road

CENTURY 21
Westbury
1085 Old Country Road

Restaurants for Garden City, Carle Place, Westbury
Café Baci
Westbury
1636 Old Country Road

Panera Bread
Carle Place
Carle Place Commons
165 Old Country Road

OYSTER BAY, LOCUST VALLEY, GLEN COVE
ANNIE SEZ

Glen Cove
121 School Street

NEXT TO NEW
Oyster Bay
59 West Main Street

WORTH REPEATING
Locust Valley
83 Birch Hill Road

ONE LAST LOOK
Locust Valley
37 Forest Avenue

Restaurants for Oyster Bay, Locust Valley

Wild Honey
Oyster Bay
1 East Main Street

Jack Halyards
Oyster Bay
62 South Street

Buckrum Stables
Locust Valley
31 Forest Avenue

JERICHO, HUNTINGTON

DSW SHOES
Jericho
1819 East Jericho Turnpike

MARSHALLS
Huntington
839 New York Avenue

FOX'S
Huntington
379 New York Avenue

COMMUNITY THRIFT
Huntington
247 New York Avenue

SECOND CHANCE
Huntington
276 Main Street

Restaurant for Huntington

Black & Blue Seafood Chophouse
Huntington
65 Wall Street

CLOTHING SIZES & CONVERSIONS

WOMEN'S CLOTHING

US	UK	ITALY	FRANCE	JAPAN
2	4	36	32	5
4	6	48	34	7
6	8	40	36	9
8	10	42	38	11
10	12	44	40	13
12	14	46	42	15
14	16		44	17
16	18			19
18	20			21

WOMEN'S SHOES

US	UK	EUROPE
4	2-1/2	35
5	3-1/2	37
6	4-1/2	38
7	5-1/2	39
8	6-1/2	40
9	7-1/2	41

NOTES

"Fashion anticipates, and elegance is a state of mind . . . a mirror of the time in which we live, a translation of the future, and should never be static."
-Oleg Cassini

INDEX

Alexis	39
All About Trendz - All About Jewelry	49
Amsterdam Boutique	31
Annie Sez	16
Arthritis Thrift Shop	91
Ayazmoon Fabric	102
B & Q	103
Beacon's Closet	88
Bijoux Terner	128
Bis Designer Resale	71
Bridal Garden	64
Buffalo Exchange	90
Canal Street	116
Cantelle Fashion Ltd.	38
Century 21 Department Stores	2
Collette	78
Community Thrift Shop	97
Conway Stores	34
Corner Closet	77
Council Thrift Shop	91
Daytona Trimming	103
Design By Nova	67
Designer Resale	72
Diamond District - 47TH Street	60
Drango Sphere Inc.	53
DSW	43
Dzhavael Couture	38
Earrings Plaza	50
Edith Machinist	85
Eli & Company	39
Encore - Premier Consignment Shop	71
Forever Fashion of NYC	53
Forever 21	24
Fox's	6
Gentlemen's Resale	72
Grenville Boys & Girls Club Sale	109

H&M	20
Hai's Trimming Inc.	103
Hat Cessory	57
Housing Works	92
Jewelry House	51
Junior League Thrift Shop	96
Kleinfeld	65
Know Style	36
La Boutique Resale	72
Last Call - Neiman Marcus	122
Lotus Vintage	86
Manhattan Worldwide Inc.	51
Manny's Millinery Supply	57
Marmalade	84
Marshalls	11
Memorial Sloan Kettering Cancer Center Thrift Shop	91
Michael's - Consignment Shop For Women	66, 70
MJM Designer Shoes	42
Mood Fabrics	101
Mystique	32
Narnia	85
Necessary Clothing	36
Next To New	75
Nima	51
Norlha	52
One Last Look	75
Paron West / Paron Annex	101
Peachfrog	18
Perla Designs	51
P & K Jewelry	52
Posh Sale at the Lighthouse	108
Prime Fabrics	102
Revival	76
RK Bridal	66

Saks Fifth Avenue - Off Fifth 123
Second Time Around 74
Shinetrim 68
Silver Tree & Cherry 50
S.M. Perfume 54
Soiffer Haskin 114
Spandex House 102
Starlight Jewelry Company 61
Stella Dallas 84
Strawberry 29
Swimwear Anywhere 124
Sylvia Pines Uniquities 85

Tanger Outlet - Riverhead 125
10 Ft. Single by Stella Dallas 84
T.J. Maxx 8
Top Button 114
TopShop 33

Unique Thrift 94
U. S. Jewelry House Ltd. 50

Vila 51
Vintage Clothing & Antique Textile
Show & Sale 83

Weavers Fabric 101
Woodbury Common Outlets 124
Worth Repeating 76

ORDER FORM

THE FASHIONISTA'S SHOPPING GUIDE TO THE GALAXY OF DISCOUNT NEW YORK FASHION
makes a great gift!!

SHIP TO:
    Name: _____
    Address: _____
    City/Town: _____
    State: _____Zip Code: _____
    Email: _____

Quantity		Price	Total
	x	$14.99 =	_____
Free Shipping (domestically)			_____
Grand total			_____

Payable to Sharyne Wolfe by check or money order.
Email me at fashionistasshoppingguide@gmail.com for multiple copy rates and international rates.

SEND PAYMENT TO:
Fashionista's Guide/Sharyne Wolfe
136 Roger Canoe Hollow
Mill Neck, New York 11765

Payment can also be made through Paypal at the website:
http://www.fashionistasshoppingguidetodiscountfashion.com/

If this is a gift would you like a gift card included?
Message:
_____
_____
_____

"A day without shopping is like a day without sunshine. Put a little sunshine in your life. Shop till you drop"
- Sharyne Wolfe

NOTES

Fashion should be a form of escapism and not a form of imprisonment"
-Alexander McQueen

NOTES

"Give a girl the correct footwear and she can conquer the world."
-Bette Midler

Made in the USA
San Bernardino, CA
25 April 2015